THE GREAT BALANCING ACT

Finding Joy as a Woman, Wife, and Mother

by

Pat Harrison

Harrison House
Tulsa, Oklahoma

06 05 04 03 02 / 10 9 8 7 6 5 4 3 2 1

The Great Balancing Act:
Finding Joy as a Woman, Wife, and Mother
ISBN 1-57794-429-1
(Former ISBN 0-89274-315-8)
Copyright © 2002 by Patsy G. Harrison
P. O. Box 35443
Tulsa, Oklahoma 74153

Published by Harrison House, Inc.
P. O. Box 35035
Tulsa, Oklahoma 74153

Contents

INTRODUCTION

Maybe you feel pulled in every direction by family, community, work, and church. You may constantly struggle to retain some sense of yourself as an individual and to find some time for just you and God.

I call it "the great balancing act," and I have had to do some tricky balancing myself over the years. I assure you there is joy to be found in meeting this challenge. As you begin to fulfill your God-ordained role as a woman of God, you will open the door wide for God to work miracles in your life according to the promises in His Word.

We are going to explore what the Word has to say about your role as a woman, wife, and mother. This study can profit you whether you are single, married, or divorced. Many of the principles we will discuss apply to you as a woman of God, regardless of your marital status.

For instance, if you are single now, perhaps you will be a wife and mother in the future. If your children are already grown and have moved away from home, you can learn principles from this book that will minister life to your children and grandchildren, as well as to younger women.

You will find this subject to be pertinent even if you never marry, because there will always be women you can minister to based on the scriptural knowledge you gain. As you help other women realize how beautiful it is that God created them as women, that one realization in itself will settle many of their problems.

Whatever your season in life, open your heart and receive. You're about to discover vital truths that can change your life as you realize the God-ordained role of a woman, a wife, and a mother!

—*Pat Harrison*

Part 1

A Woman by Birth

1

FREE TO BECOME
WHO YOU ARE IN CHRIST

You have a big responsibility to function in the home as a godly wife and mother, but you must first learn to be who you are in Christ. You must accept the fact that God created you as a woman. Since He created you that way, you can know that you are able to function in the role of a godly woman exactly as He intended you to function.

You are a woman by birth. Psalm 139:14 KJV says, "I will praise thee; for I am fearfully and wonderfully made: marvellous are thy works; and that my soul knoweth right well." God does not make mistakes. Rejoice that He skillfully crafted you as a woman.

You must understand that it is okay to be the unique individual God has created you to be. The best way I know to explain that statement is to use my own life as an example.

I personally had a difficult time learning that it was all right to be me. When I was younger, I was a shy, introverted person who could easily be intimidated. I set no boundaries with others, so people felt free to walk all over me. I would never say anything; I would just step back out of the way and go on.

The saddest part about it all was that I liked it that way. I enjoyed staying in the background, where I did not have to be seen or heard. No one had to know who I was, and I was not required to do anything I did not want to do. The root of that desire was selfishness, and it produced a negative harvest.

It is not fun to be a shy, introverted person, because intimidation is always accompanied by fear. Fear is torment, and torment is not fun.

I was even afraid to go up to someone new and introduce myself. The thought of doing that could frighten me to tears. As a result, everyone thought I was snobbish and conceited. If they only knew.

I could not function the way I needed to as long as fear and torment ruled in my life. That meant I had some learning to do. I had to find out that it was okay to be who I was and to set boundaries. I had to learn what I liked, what I did not like, and how I wanted things to be according to the Word of God. I had to allow the Word of God and the Holy Spirit to change *me*.

I did not know all that when my husband, Buddy, and I were first married. During the first few years of our marriage, Buddy was out of fellowship with the Lord, and we were not living for God as we should have been.

I prayed selfishly for Buddy, saying, "God, change him." Every time I would get down on my knees with that prayer, the Lord would say, *Pat, you need to change.*

I would always protest. *"Me? But what about...?"*

The Lord would always stop me short and say, *It's not about him; it's about you.*

My flesh did not like it when God talked to me about my need to change. Nevertheless, I knew it was true. I had so much to learn in order to allow God to work in me.

At the same time, God was working in Buddy. The Lord desired for Buddy and me to allow Him to work in us and cause us to become what He had created us to be so the two of us could come together as a complete force for His kingdom. What mattered to God was not how *I* wanted Buddy to change, but what *God* wanted to do in him. In the same way, God was concerned that I change, not according to Buddy's expectations, but according to His plan and purpose for my life.

In that process, I began to learn that it was okay to be myself. Little by little, I discovered that God was first in my life and that Buddy was not my source.

That is where many women trip up. A wife can be all caught up in trying to please the man she loves. When she realizes she is not doing what he thinks she should be doing, she tries to do everything within her power to be what he wants her to be. It will never be enough, because she tries to change in her own strength. She desires to be something she is not and will never be, because that is not what God intended.

Focus on pleasing God first. God intended for you to live your life on this earth as a selfless person, mature in the things of God. Therefore, He expects you to allow the Holy Spirit and the Word of God to work in you and change you into that person He says you are in Christ. When you do that, you please Him. In addition, when you are pleasing to the Father, you will be pleasing to those around you.

I can use the relationship between Buddy and his dad as an example. For years, they never got along. It did not matter what Buddy did; it was not good enough for his dad.

Then one day, Buddy said, "I've had enough of this. Dad is never going to think I can do anything worthwhile."

I replied, "Well, just pray for God's guidance and let Him work in you."

That is what Buddy did. He quit thinking about trying to please his father and concentrated instead on obeying what God had called him to do. Once he did that, his dad became pleased with him. Suddenly he thought Buddy was the most wonderful thing God ever created.

Buddy began to learn who he was in God. He became determined to be the man God had called him to be, no matter what anyone else thought about it.

I had to come to that same place on another level. I had always had a great relationship with my parents, but I still had to learn how to overcome some unhealthy mindsets I had developed over the years that always made me feel second best or "never quite good enough."

Since Buddy and I married at a very young age, I had to learn how to overcome those mindsets within the context of marriage. For instance, I had to learn that it was okay for me to get upset or angry at times, as long as I did not sin in my anger.

Thank God, I have a faithful, merciful, longsuffering God. Over a period of years, I learned how to set boundaries. I discovered how to think highly of myself as a child of God.

Frame Your World With Your Mouth

I learned in those early years that God had to be first in my life. It was not an easy lesson to learn. I certainly did not learn it overnight, but I continued to allow God to work in me. I continued to listen to the Holy Spirit and cry out to God for many long hours in my prayer closet.

Today I can say with certainty, it was worth it. It made me a better person and helped me become the person God had created me to be.

I no longer asked God to change Buddy in ways I thought my husband should change. Instead, I prayed, "God, this is a situation I don't know how to pray about, but by the Holy Spirit I will pray the perfect prayer for my husband. The answer to that prayer will be right, and it will be good."

Nine times out of ten, I would pray through that particular situation and experience a release. During the time of prayer, God would take me to Scriptures I could confess over my husband in faith. I had prayed the perfect prayer, and in my heart I believed God's Word. Therefore, I knew I was actually framing my world with the Word I was confessing with my mouth.

Buddy and I celebrated our fortieth wedding anniversary in October 1998. He went home to be with the Lord in November of that same year. That was one of the hardest days of my life, but it was still good because God had not left me. He was still with me and was still my Source. I experienced the supernatural peace that only my loving Lord could give to sustain me.

The Word of God was strong within me, and I spoke out that Word as I had done so many times before. There was strength in those life-giving words. I was strong, not in myself, but in the Word and in my Father God.

You, too, can frame your world with your words of faith. In any situation you face, you can confess the Word and see God's promises become reality.

You must come to understand and accept what God has specifically called you to do in this life before you can fulfill your role as a godly wife and mother.

When God first began to let me know that He had called me to preach the Word, I thought, *God, You have to be kidding. I just can't do that. I can't even stand up and give a testimony, because I shake so much that my voice quivers. Everyone knows I'm scared out of my wits to get up in front of people and speak!*

The Lord calmly responded, *You're looking at the wrong person.*

I knew what God meant. I was not looking to Him for my strength. That was the end of that discussion, but it took me awhile to settle within myself that I could do what God had created and called me to do. God knew my heart was to walk in His will. I wanted my will to be His will. He kept working with me as I came around the block repeatedly, each time a little closer.

Finally, I said, "Okay, Lord. I have prayed since I was a little girl that I want to know You better. I want so much for my will to be Your will. So I know I can do this because You're asking me to." When I yielded my will to the Father's will, my spirit became open to the Holy Spirit, and He began to work in me and through me.

God was so gracious to me the first time I stood up to speak. It was at a small ladies' meeting, and my audience was a group of precious, gentle, older ladies who couldn't have cared less how many mistakes I made. They were there to hear the truth I had to share with them and to love on me.

After my message, the women all came up and told me how well I had done, because they had the love of God in their hearts. My message may not have been the best they had ever heard, but they had enough sense to know it was important to encourage me as I stepped out in faith to obey God.

God will never tell you to do something and then abandon you once you begin it. When you act on what He has called you to do, He always puts you where you will receive the encouragement you need to keep growing.

The most difficult change for me came later in ministry when God began to change the anointing I operated in. Before this time, Buddy and I had always ministered together in tongues and interpretation and in prophecy. God began to deal with me that I needed to move more in the prophetic anointing He had placed on my life.

However, as I began to step out and minister in that prophetic anointing within the church where Buddy and I were the pastors, some of the people in the congregation came against me. They would talk to each other about me, saying that I was beginning to have a hard spirit. When I would speak a prophetic word of direction by the unction of the Holy Spirit, they would say I was just speaking my own words, trying to get my own way.

I prayed, "God, I've had it. If this is the way Your people are, I don't want any part of it. I'm not doing anything else!" So I sat down and stopped actively ministering in the church.

We're all human beings, and no matter what kind of responsibility God has given us, we've all had to go through some hard times that have helped us grow and mature so we could fulfill our responsibilities. For each one of us, God's desire is to bring us to a place in our spiritual walk where we allow the Holy Spirit and the Word of God to continually work in us and change us into the image of Jesus.

After I stopped ministering in the church, I began to experience some health problems. After a while, I could not even go to church because I was in too much pain. This condition led to a bout of depression.

I had never suffered from depression before, nor had I ever seen anyone else in depression. At first, I did not know what I was dealing with. During that time, a really good day for me was to get up out of my bed, walk across my bedroom floor, and sit in the bedroom chair.

I thought, *God, what have I done to myself?* I knew I had brought this adversity on myself. Nevertheless, I continued to do what I knew to do. I read the Word and prayed in the Spirit. As I lay in bed and prayed, sometimes it seemed like my prayers bounced off the bedroom wall and came back to hit me in the face.

I had gotten myself into this mess, but I could not get myself out. I knew it was going to take others praying for me to pull me out of this pit I was in.

I prayed, "God, I thank You for calling on those who will hear You to pray for me because I can't help myself at this point. I got myself in this mess, but I can't help myself get out of it."

God answered that prayer. I began to receive little notes from people that said, "I don't know you, and you don't know me. But I sensed I needed to write you this note and let you know I'm praying for you." People did that because God understood that I needed to know my prayer was being answered.

This time of depression was not something I had to do. I brought it on myself. It all started when I resisted what God had specifically called me to do for His kingdom. Instead of stepping out in faith to walk in that call, I had opened the door through disobedience, and the devil was working in my life to steal my health and peace of mind.

Thank God, I had enough sense to cry out to God and ask Him to lead other people to pray for me and pull me out of my mess. I had sunk too low in depression, but no matter how low I seemed to sink, I was always aware of God's love. He never left me. I always knew He was there.

I continued to do what I knew to do. I continued to say, "God, thank You for Your help. Thank You for loving me. I know You're working in me, and I *want* You to work in me. Help me discern where I've opened myself up to the devil so I can close that door. And, Lord, help me discern the work You are completing in me so I don't close that door."

God is such a loving Father. He will always help you in time of need. All you have to do is ask Him. God began to give me understanding in these matters. It took several months for me to come out of that depression, but when I did, I was a different person. God had performed the final phase of the work He had begun several years before that, changing me from a shy, introverted person into the bold, extroverted person He had always intended for me to be.

That does not mean God totally changed my personality. There are still times I want to slip back and become shy and introverted again. I recognize that temptation and tell myself, *No, I don't go there anymore.*

Freedom from fear was the biggest change that took place in me. I was free from what other people thought of me. I was free from others' words that tried to place me in a box of religious thinking and tell me what kind of person I should be.

For instance, when Buddy and I first began to pastor, I was on the PTA committee for the school my girls attended at that time. One day at a PTA meeting, I was talking to two of the women I had befriended on the committee. When I told them that my husband and I had just started a church, one of the women exclaimed, "You mean your husband is a pastor?"

"Yes," I replied.

"Oh, my! You don't look or act *anything* like a pastor's wife!"

I thought, *Well, praise God. I'm so glad I don't fit your stereotype of a pastor's wife.*

Religious people have their own ideas of the way a pastor's wife should behave, what she should look like, what she should do, and how she should function. Those ideas are not necessarily scriptural.

The important thing is that you live according to what God has called you to do, no matter what people think. Your responsibility is to discern and then act on what God is saying to you.

Be free to become who you are in God. You will be a testimony, both to your family members and to those outside the home.

I was glad I did not fit inside that woman's "pastor's wife" box, because I am not a mold that man has made. I am a creation of God. He saw fit to create me as a woman because He knew I could function in that role the way He wanted me to.

God does everything with purpose. He did not create you as a woman by accident. He knew that you as a woman would be able to *be* everything He intended you to be and *do* everything He intended for you to do.

You must allow the Word of God and the Holy Spirit to work in you so you can grow and mature in the Lord and become the person God has called you to be in every arena of life.

You have to come to that same place in your life before you can ever fulfill your scriptural role as a godly woman. When you become a little anxious about what God is asking you to do, speak out your faith: "Anxiousness is not of God. I will not have anxiety. I have the peace of God. I operate in the love, peace, and joy of the Holy Spirit." That is one way you can allow the Holy Spirit to work in you.

However, let me give you a quick word of caution that we'll discuss in more detail later: Once you become a wife and mother, you must always be careful to keep your priorities straight. Whatever God has called you to do for His kingdom, even if He has called you to the ministry, that call is not to be above your home. Your home and your family must be taken care of first. If you are putting your ministry before your husband and children, you are not in the will of God.

So many women do not want to hear that. They say, "Well, bless God, I know what God has said to me."

But do they really? That haughty spirit makes me question whether they have really heard from God. You need to seek Jesus until His love flows through you and supernatural peace regarding His call on your life floods your heart. Then you can walk in His timing, and no one is damaged. Then everyone is brought into complete harmony as you fulfill what God has asked you to do.

Equipped To Fulfill His Will

It is so important that you function in this life as the woman God created you to be. He has made you a unique creation. There are certain things God has specifically called *you* to be and to do on this earth.

That is why it is so important for you to obtain the truth. God has not called you to be someone you cannot be. He would never ask you to do anything without giving you the equipment and the ability you need to complete the task.

As you have probably already found out, things do not just automatically happen the way you want them to in life. You have to work at it. You have to learn. You have to dig into the Word of God to gain understanding. Then through the revelation and understanding you receive from the Word, you can begin to be true to who you are in God.

When you know that your actions are in line with God's Word and that you are doing what God has called you to do, you can walk in peace. You can know "I'm following God; I'm faithful to my commitment to be all God has called me to be. Therefore, I'm free to become who I am in Christ."

2

Live Life as a Woman of God

The first man and woman walked in the Garden of Eden as two perfect creations of God. They were suitable, pleasant, and fully adapted to their purpose—fellowship with their Creator. In fact the phrase in verse 31 of Genesis 1 "and, behold, it was very good" emphasizes the perfection of everything God made.[1]

The Bible tells us that God placed both the Tree of Life and the Tree of Knowledge of Good and Evil in the midst of the Garden. Adam and Eve could freely partake of every tree, including the Tree of Life at any time, as often as they wanted (Gen. 2:16), except the scholars agree that the Tree of Knowledge of Good and Evil represents human autonomy and independence from God—the old "I-did-it-my-way" spirit.[2]

If Adam and Eve had obeyed God in the Garden, they would have retained their perfection, the state of harmony and wholeness and oneness with God. When they decided to disobey

God's Word and live life by their own rules, they stepped away from the will of God. Thus, they lost their perfection.

What Adam and Eve lost, Jesus restored. Hebrews 10:10 KJV says, "By the which will we are sanctified through the offering of the body of Jesus Christ once for all." Verse 14 tells us, "for by one offering he hath perfected for ever them that are sanctified."

> Whom we preach, warning every man, and teaching every man in all wisdom; that we may present every man perfect in Christ Jesus (Col. 1:28 KJV).

You could say that Jesus is our Tree of Life. Jesus told the disciples, "I am the way, the truth and the life. No one comes to the Father except through me" (John 14:6). When we accept Jesus and the work He did for us on the tree of Calvary (1 Pet. 2:24), He becomes a tree of life for us. He brings perfection and oneness with God that was lost in the Garden into our hearts.

Although you were born of natural parents, you can be the perfect woman God created you to be through your spiritual adoption in Jesus. It brings you into relationship and fellowship with your Creator and enables you to fulfill His purpose for your life.

As you feed upon the Word of God and fellowship with Jesus, you can dwell in that state of restored perfection as a new creation in Him. When you know who you are in Christ, you can be who He expects you to be and do all that He expects you to do. However, it is only by looking to Jesus that this is possible.

You may be thinking, *I don't feel perfect at all.* You cannot walk by what you feel; you must walk by faith in Jesus and what the Bible says. (Gal. 2:20.) The longer you walk by faith, the more your feelings will align with the Word.

According to John 1, Jesus and the Word of God are the same. The more you read and study the Bible, the more the Lord—Father, Son, and Holy Spirit—will be revealed to you. God's Word gives light and understanding. (Ps. 119:30.) The Word will provide a clear understanding of the Lord and you will gain a greater knowledge of who you are and what you have through Jesus' death, burial, and resurrection.

Prior to someone's death that person makes a "last will and testament." It outlines the distribution of his worldly possessions. Maybe someone left you a million dollars in his will, but you won't know it unless you read the will. The same is true with the Bible.

The Bible is called the Old and New Testaments. It is the revealed will of God for His people. It is the distribution of God's "goods" for those who have accepted Jesus. As you read the Bible, you will discover God, His plans for your life, and all He has made available to you.

God says that when you accepted Jesus, you became a new creation. (2 Cor. 5:17.) Your spirit, the real you, became perfect at that moment because you received God's nature, and *He* is perfect. Your spirit within you is the part of you that enables you to function as God created you to on this earth. You begin to realize the truth and walk in it as you continually spend time in His Word.

That is why it is so important to meditate on the Word; it keeps you aware of who you are in Jesus Christ so you can walk in that reality. On the other hand, if you *don't* meditate on what the Word says about you, the Christian walk can become a drudgery instead of a joy. You may begin to wonder, *Why is it so hard for me to live for the Lord?*

The truth is, you have lost your awareness of the Word. You have not let its promises work inside of you until you are aware of who you are in Jesus Christ every moment of every day. In Joshua 1:8, the Lord says that awareness of the Word—speaking, meditating, and doing it—is vital to your success and prosperity.

This book of the law shall not depart out of thy mouth [speaking]; but thou shalt meditate [thinking] therein day and night, that thou mayest observe to do [doing] according to all that is written therein: for then thou shalt make thy way prosperous, and then thou shalt have good success (Josh. 1:8 KJV).

What we see, hear, and think about is what we do. If we see, hear, and think negativity, then negativity is produced in our lives. If we focus on all that is true, honest, just, pure, lovely, of a good report, virtuous, and worthy of praise (Phil. 4:8), we become aware of those things and do them.

Confess what the Word says about who you are in Christ. Then as you hear it, it will penetrate your heart and become a reality. As you speak out God's promise, the day will come when the manifestation is complete. However, just like the food you eat, the Word will only become a part of you as you feed on it continually.

Food does not give you the strength and nourishment you need if you just sit and look at it every breakfast, lunch, and dinner. You have to eat the food if it is going to do you any good. Only then will the food become a part of your body. This is why health experts place such an emphasis on eating balanced meals and nutritious foods.

In the same way, it is important that you eat a balanced diet of God's Word, which is food to your spirit. As you do, you give your spirit the wisdom and strength needed to fulfill God's purpose for you as a godly woman.

Too many Christians are starving their spirits by neglecting the Word. They look at a passage of Scripture and say, "I don't know what that means. I don't understand that." Then they put their Bibles back on the shelves and never apply the Scriptures to their lives.

That is as foolish as sitting down at the dinner table and saying, "Well, I don't understand why I have to sit here and look at this food. It isn't doing me any good."

You are being ridiculous if you look at your Bible that gathers dust on the shelf and then wonder why the Christian life is so difficult to live.

You have to pick the Bible up and find out what it says for it to have any effect in your life. Continually meditate on God's promises, confessing them with your mouth.

It's a decision that only you can make. You have to choose to let God's Word become a part of you, knowing that it isn't just paper and ink, but it is life. The Word is a part of who God created you to be.

Get Acquainted With the Holy Spirit

Another thing you must do to become the woman God created you to be is to know the Holy Spirit. The Holy Spirit's purpose in your life is to do a work in you. He wants to lead you into a higher walk with God so you can fulfill your divine destiny on the earth.

In order for that to take place, you must learn how to hear the voice of the Holy Spirit.

For example, how will you know where you should plant your next financial seed? You will have to discern the leading of the Holy Spirit.

Certain seeds are designed to produce certain harvests in your life according to your faith. When you have faith in God and you know the voice of the Holy Spirit, He will direct you to plant in fields that will reap an abundant, multiplied harvest for you.

But that opportunity will be lost to you if you fail to make the effort to know the Holy Spirit. When you know His voice, you can be confident that you hear clearly what God instructs you to do. Through the Word and prayer you will discover wisdom.

As you cultivate your relationship with the Holy Spirit, you will come to a place in your spiritual walk where you know instantly when He speaks to you. No longer will you miss divine opportunities because of wasted time spent wondering, *Was that You, God?* Whether the Spirit of God speaks to you through the Word, through another person, through prophecy, or through your private time of prayer with Him, faith will immediately arise in your heart to do what He has asked you to do. An intimate knowledge of both the Word and the Holy Spirit is the prerequisite to living successfully as a woman of God. It is the only way you can tap into your God-given ability to walk in wisdom in every area of life.

Proverbs 3:17 says that all the ways of God's wisdom are pleasantness and peace. If you are experiencing supernatural peace and pleasantness in a certain area of your life, you can know that you are walking in the full wisdom of God in that area. If that is not the case, turn your attention toward God and seek Him through prayer and the Word. He will show you the changes you need to make in order to walk in His wisdom and experience His peace.

From the Word of God we learn that we need both the Spirit and the Word to live as God intends us to live. In 2 Corinthians 3:6, the apostle Paul writes, "Who also hath made us able ministers of the New Testament; not of the letter, but of the spirit: for the letter killeth, but the spirit giveth life."

As a Pharisee, Saul, who became Paul, knew the law and every jot and tittle of the Old Testament. (Gal.1:14; Phil. 3:4-6.) Without Jesus and the Holy Spirit in His life, he did not understand the spirit of the law; thus, he persecuted and killed Christians. (Acts 8:1-3; 9:1-2; Gal. 1:13.) Once he was saved and baptized in the Holy Spirit, he could understand the truth, the spirit of God's law, and how to properly apply it. (Acts 9:3-18.)

If you abide in the Word and maintain a strong prayer life, you will stand immovable in your faith just as Jesus was immovable. If you do not spend regular time in conversation with the Lord, His Word becomes just a dead letter to you and your Christian walk becomes nothing more than dead works.

Living for God requires spending much time in both the Word *and* in prayer. It is very important to have a strong prayer life. It is also important to know the Word of God so it can be effective in you. The key is to find a balance between these two vital elements of your walk with God.

One way you find that balance is to speak forth the Word you have already planted in your heart when you talk to the Father in prayer. Prayer is not telling God all your problems. Prayer is a two-way communication with God based on His Word.

You speak forth the Word to Him during your time in prayer, and He responds to it by bringing His Word to pass in your life according to your faith. Each answer that is manifested builds a confidence in you that says, "Yes, what God says is so, and He will do what He says He will do."

This is far different than thinking, *If I confess this promise a hundred times, I'll receive it.* A person who does that depends on works rather than on faith in God's Word.

As you make it a practice to study and meditate on the Word, it becomes a part of you. Then as you pray to the Father, the Spirit of God within you will rise up and give you the understanding, the revelation knowledge, and the strength you need to stand strong in faith until your answer is manifested. When that happens, the works will naturally flow out of your fellowship and communication with God.

The Word and prayer are equally important. They have to work together. God created us for fellowship, so fellowship in prayer is vital for our spiritual growth. He gave us the written Word so we could have the guidelines to ensure that our fellowship and intimacy with God come forth and are revealed in this world to His glory.

You can attain God's highest in this life. First, become a woman of the Word and of prayer for your Creator. Second, do it for the man God gives you, for as you will see later, you were created for him and not he for you. Finally, do it for your own spiritual fulfillment as a woman of God.

Just this one principle alone can change your life if you will act on it. As you continually feed on the Word and speak it forth in your prayer time with the Lord, the life-giving power of the Holy Spirit will begin to work mightily within you. He will help you see different areas of your life in which you can take hold of

God's principles and change things you may have struggled with for years.

Cultivate a Desire To Know Him

To reach this place of intimacy with the Father God, you are going to have to work at it. You do not just say, "Praise God, I'm born again; therefore, I'm fixed." No, you have to mature and grow in your fellowship with God as you allow the Holy Spirit to do a work in you.

When I say you have to work at your relationship with God, I do not mean you have to struggle with it. You will have to cultivate a strong desire to be totally engulfed by the presence of Jesus.

Work the Word of God in your life, and go often to the throne room of the Father. Develop an intimate relationship with Him so you can know Him and not just know about Him.

Consider the example of Moses. Moses witnessed all kinds of miracles in his life. Nevertheless, the one desire of his heart was to know God. In Exodus 33:18 KJV, Moses pled with the Lord, "I beseech thee, shew me thy glory."

We can also find this same heart desire in the New Testament. The apostle Paul had seen God perform all kinds of spectacular miracles. But Paul had a passion to know Jesus and to discover what brings joy to His heart:

> That I may know him, and the power of his resurrection, and the fellowship of his sufferings, being made conformable unto his death (Phil. 3:10 KJV).

Hebrews 11:6 KJV gives you another vital key to attaining God's highest as a woman of God:

> But without faith it is impossible to please him: for he that cometh to God must believe that he is, and that *he is a rewarder of them that diligently seek him.*

You cannot please God without faith. When you come before the Lord in prayer, you must believe that He is and that He is a rewarder.

The key to this verse is the phrase "of them that diligently seek Him." Diligence to seek Him, to obey Him, and to walk in the things of God will bring God's rewards into your life. You have to discipline yourself to be diligent. Maintaining that determination is very difficult if we try to go the way of the world, because discipline has become such a foreign term to most people.

The theme that permeates modern society is "I'm not responsible." People want to disclaim any personal responsibility. Instead, they want the government to do everything for them. Then if something goes wrong, it is not their fault. It is the government's fault.

This same attitude has crept into the body of Christ. Christians have the attitude, "I'm not responsible for not receiving the answer to my prayer. God said He would do it, and He didn't do it. It's His responsibility, not mine."

You are responsible for your own spiritual growth, just as you are responsible to feed and clothe yourself, to keep yourself clean, and to do whatever else is necessary to grow and mature in the natural. Your ability to walk in God's blessings grows as you fellowship with Him daily in the Word and in prayer, diligently seeking Him regarding the manner in which He would have you live in this world.

Now, you may say, "But I just don't have time to spend hours alone with God every day." Christians often are hung up on this point. They mistakenly think that the only way they can diligently seek God is to find a special place to go to every day where they can spend three or more hours praying in the Spirit. Then they think of their busy lives and become discouraged, saying, "But I don't have a special place, and I don't have three hours to pray."

The devil would like nothing more than for Christians to think that way. He knows that those who become discouraged will ultimately not pray or exercise the Word much at all.

The truth is, you do not have to find a special place to fellowship with God. When you have been feeding the Word into your spirit, you can open your mouth and speak it forth anywhere you happen to be. So open your mouth and speak the Word. It does not matter whether you're in the shower, in the car, or at your desk. Wherever you are, open your mouth.

I enjoy my special time with the Lord in the morning. I always get up earlier than I need to so I can have that time with Him—not because I have to, but because I want to. He is my life. With all my heart, I desire to spend time with Him.

Some of my best times of dancing and shouting in the Holy Spirit are in the shower. I like to use that time to build myself up, praying in the Spirit and speaking forth the Word of God that is alive in me. As I fellowship with God in this way, it brings a joy and exuberance that I carry with me for the rest of the day.

Take Care of Yourself Physically

I have talked to you at length about taking care of your spiritual life so you can walk in the fullness of God's plan for you as a woman of God. However, it is also very important that you take care of yourself physically.

God wants you to take pleasure in your body in a godly sense. Knowing that God created you to be a woman, you can take pride in keeping your body in good condition so it can function properly as God made it to function.

That means you first have to keep your body clean, and feed your body the right kind of food. If your diet is unbalanced and unhealthy, your body will not function properly. You need to exercise regularly; otherwise, your muscles and tendons will not be strong and firm the way they should be.

God gave you skin that is perfect, but you need to take care of it. Do not look at blemishes and say, "Well, that's just the way I am." No, you need to find out what you can do to improve the health of your skin.

You need to take pride in how you look, how you carry yourself, and how you care for your body. Your body is the temple of the Holy Spirit. (1 Cor. 3:16.) You should not want your temple, the actual dwelling place of the Holy Spirit, to be shabby, unhealthy, or out of shape.

Imagine a man who in the natural is the epitome of physical strength and courage—someone the Bible might call "a mighty man of valor." Now try to imagine such a man consenting to live in a rundown, unpainted, about-to-fall-down shack with no material comforts. He does nothing to better his situation; instead, he just sits there and wonders, *I'm a mighty man of valor, so why am I living this way?*

That is difficult to imagine. It should be just as difficult to imagine yourself with a rundown, out-of-shape body. You have all the ability of the Greater One within you. You are a king and a priest unto God. Your body is a temple of the Most High.

When you think of a temple, you probably visualize a work of beauty—something that has been skillfully and carefully handcrafted to give honor to the One who is to be worshiped within. In the same way, it brings honor to God when you take care of *your* temple, making sure that you look and feel your best as you live your life for Him.

Of course, that does not mean you are to spend all your time on your outward appearance. As you choose the Word first, God will help you find the right balance between spiritual and natural pursuits. Even though exercising and caring for your body don't profit you as much as developing your spirit, it is still your responsibility to take good care of yourself physically.

Consider the position you are in as a Christian woman. So many people around you do not understand spiritual things and therefore make judgments according to your natural, outward appearance. That is why the "natural you" that everyone sees should radiate outwardly with health and vitality even as the beauty of Jesus shines forth from within.

When you know you are taking care of yourself physically the way you should, you can then say, "God gave me this body. I am taking care of it, and I know He is proud. He's concerned with every area of my life, so I know I bring joy and pleasure to Him when I am a good steward of this temple of the Holy Spirit."

Now, I want to give you a word of caution here. It is a known fact that the world takes everything to excess. Today, we are bombarded with the message to "exercise, exercise, exercise." All we see on television and in magazines and catalogs are images of *very* thin people who are supposed to be our standard for looking beautiful.

I know I will never look like those thin actresses and models, no matter how much weight I lose. I am just not built like that. I went through school as skinny as a rail, and that condition holds no appeal to me. I do not want any more of the ridicule I experienced back then, when I was called names like "Olive Oil" and "Bird Legs." It took me a while to get over all that teasing I endured when I was a girl.

Perhaps you were teased as you grew up because of some aspect of your physical appearance. If so, it is important to deal with any leftover hurts you still have because of those thoughtless words.

You must realize that many kids are just rude. They are not restricted by a sense of consideration for others, so they say what they think.

The rude comments of others may have made you self-conscious about your body in the past, but you can decide today not to let those words keep you in bondage any longer. Remember, old things have passed away and new things have come because you are a new creation in Christ! (2 Cor. 5:17.) You must decide how much exercise you should have or what kind of food you should eat. There is no single, perfect standard for everyone. Just find out what is right for you as an individual. Do what you know to do to take care of your body.

For instance, at my age I cannot do an entire hour of aerobic exercise. But I *can* do thirty minutes with a little rest in between, and that is enough for me.

Tell the Lord, "Father, You have to help me. I need You to show me what I should do to get my body in the best shape I possibly can." As you seek Him for wisdom, He will give you the wisdom you need in this area, as well as in every other area of your life.

If you ever find yourself wavering in your resolve to eat right and exercise, do not get upset with yourself. Praise God, you are victorious in Christ. You may have to play a long game, but remember it is your bat and ball. You have to keep playing until you win.

Most of us are too conscious of time as we pursue the goals we've set for getting our bodies in shape. We need to remember that God doesn't operate in the realm of time. The important thing is to look at our past efforts and to realize that, in the process, we have matured as we have refused to give up. How long it takes to reach our goals is not the important thing. Rather, we should focus on the fact that we are obeying God in this area of our lives and that we will ultimately be victorious.

Here's another thing to remember regarding this issue of taking care of your body: Do not take every physical attack against your body personally. Whenever you experience symptoms of sickness, you can get off on the wrong track if you are always wondering, *Oh, no. What door have I opened to the enemy?*

When Satan comes against your body and you experience symptoms, you don't have to spend a lot of time questioning in your mind, *Where have I opened the door?* You will know immediately if you've opened the door to the enemy because the Holy Spirit will make it known to you. If you don't have that immediate inner knowing, you can rest assured that the physical attack you're experiencing is just Satan coming to steal the Word from you.

He is just after the Word. This has been true from the beginning. Satan has always wanted to exalt himself above the Word. He thinks if he can just get at the Word on the inside of you, he will be a little bit closer to destroying you.

You can see how foolish the devil is. He has deceived himself so much, he does not realize that the power of God will always be more powerful than any power he has at his disposal. He may try to convince you that he knows what he's talking about, but you know better because you know the Word.

At the first sign of a physical attack on your body, just go to the Father and speak His Word to Him. Say, "Father, I know You will help me in this because You made my natural body the same way You made my spirit on the inside of me. You know all the workings and functions of this natural body, so I want to thank You for giving me the knowledge and understanding I need to receive my healing and get my body in good shape."

When you determine to keep your body subjected to the Word of God, it has no choice but to conform. However, you have to get into the Word and let God's wisdom become revelation knowledge to you.

Be an Example of a Godly Woman

Now, you don't set that goal for yourself because you're a vain, prideful person. You do it because you know you are to be an example to others.

There are people watching you. This is the reason you should be so very careful in making sure everything you do follows in the footsteps of Jesus. If your life shows people a true example of a woman as God created woman to be, others will follow your example. Because of what they have seen in you, they will start down the same path you are traveling—the path to becoming whole in spirit, soul, and body.

Personally, I have made up my mind that I am going to follow Jesus. To the best of my ability, I will be the example He intends me to be both to those around me and to those I minister to.

You, too, can be the example God created you to be. The way you do this is by fellowshipping with Him on a regular basis, letting His attributes flow into you and become perfected in you. Then those same divine attributes can flow through you and out into the world.

Here is another word of caution: If you try to do any of this in your own strength, you will never do it. You have to let your will become *God's* will before His divine nature can flow through you.

If you are in God's family, you have the same characteristics He has, and those divine characteristics should be working in you. Just think of your own children. In the natural, you give life to your children, and they share your physical and personality characteristics. When you see these similarities, it thrills your heart.

The Father God is the same way. When you are an imitator of Him, it thrills His heart and brings Him joy. (Eph. 5:1.) Determine to become an imitator of God. Resolve that nothing will stop you from living as a complete, perfected woman of God from this day forward.

3

Fashioned for Fellowship

It is crucial that you learn to cultivate and grow in your fellowship with God. Toward that end, I want to give you a few guidelines that will help you avail yourself of the Holy Spirit's power and supernatural direction in your daily life.

The Holy Spirit's power is always present in every situation to provide whatever you may need. However, you have to draw on that power and allow it to work in you and through you if you want to receive the benefits of His supernatural help and guidance.

The first guideline is one I have already mentioned, but I want to discuss it a little further: You must make a practice of meditating on God's Word. In Joshua 1, God reveals the importance of this step:

> Now after the death of Moses the servant of the Lord it came to pass, that the Lord spake unto Joshua the son of Nun, Moses' minister, saying, Moses my servant is dead;

now therefore arise [take his place], go over this Jordan, thou, and all this people, unto the land which I do give to them, even to the children of Israel. Every place that the sole of your foot shall tread upon, that have I given unto you, as I said unto Moses....

There shall not any man be able to stand before thee all the days of thy life: as I was with Moses, so I will be with thee: I will not fail thee, nor forsake thee.

Only be thou strong and very courageous, that thou mayest observe to do according to all the law, which Moses my servant commanded thee: turn not from it to the right hand or to the left, that thou mayest prosper whithersoever thou goest.

This book of the law shall not depart out of thy mouth; but thou shalt meditate therein day and night, that thou mayest observe to do according to all that is written therein: for then thou shalt make thy way prosperous, and then thou shalt have good success (Josh. 1:1-3,5,7,8 KJV).

God told Joshua, "I am leading you this way, and you will experience victory if you do what I say."

Notice God said in verse 8 that it is not enough to speak His words out of your mouth. You have to meditate on them so they become a part of you. Then you are able to speak forth the Word that lives on the inside of you and frame your world as it pertains to you according to its truth.

How do you meditate on the Word? Sometimes it is helpful to think of it as worry in reverse. For instance, in the natural you might worry about your son, dwelling on thoughts like, *My son isn't doing this right, and he isn't doing that right either. When will he ever grow up? What if he gets in trouble?*

Those are thoughts of doubt and worry. But you can turn that situation around by shining the light of God's Word on it. You can replace those thoughts of worry with faith-filled confessions from God's Word about your son:

"The Word of God says that all my household will come into the kingdom of God. Jeremiah 31:16-17 says that because God has heard my prayers and has seen my weeping unto Him, all my children will escape the land of the enemy and return to the truth in which they were raised. It will be no other way, for I believe it will be as God has spoken."

This is just one of God's many promises that you can meditate on day and night in order to experience victory in this area of your life. All His promises are for you, but you have to meditate on them in order to see them happen in your life.

Another way to understand what it means to meditate on the Word is to think of a cow chewing its cud. A cow has two stomachs. It chews, chews, chews a mouthful of food, and then finally swallows it. The food enters the first stomach; then the cow brings it back up again and chews it some more. The last time the cow swallows the partially digested food, it goes into its second stomach. There the food is further digested so it can be assimilated into the cow's body, providing the nourishment and strength the cow needs to live a full life as the cow God created it to be.

In the same way, you are to "chew" on the Word by meditating on it. You must chew and chew and chew on that Word. When you first "swallow" the Word you have been meditating on, you may still be giving only mental assent to it. Then you bring that Word back up and chew on it some more—meditating on it as you go about your day.

As you continue to do that, eventually the Word you have been meditating on will go deep into your spirit and become life and strength to you.

> I will praise thee with uprightness of heart, when I shall have learned thy righteous judgments. I will keep thy statutes: O forsake me not utterly.
>
> Wherewithal shall a young man cleanse his way? by taking heed thereto according to thy word. With my whole heart have I sought thee: O let me not wander from thy commandments. Thy word have I hid in mine heart, that I might not sin against thee (Ps. 119:7-11).

While you speak forth the Word you have been meditating on in faith, you become that which God created you to be—a living epistle of God.

How To Meditate on Scripture

Personally, I like to meditate on Psalm 23:1, which says the Lord is my shepherd. Jesus is my Good Shepherd, who leads, guides, and protects me each step of the way.

I chew on that verse for a long time, meditating on the significance of every word. I start by meditating on the first word: "The." That means He is the one and only Lord. Then I meditate on the second word: "Lord." Who is the Lord? He is my Savior. He is my deliverer. He is my anointing. He is all I need. He is my everything. Next, I meditate on the third word: "is" He *is*. He is the great I Am to me.

You can do the same thing with any verse that ministers to your heart. Continue to meditate on each word of the verse in the manner I just described. Soon, that verse will become a part of you. You will get so excited about it that you will look for someone to tell that it is working in your life.

Christians often try to find excuses for not taking the time to meditate on the Word. For instance, many people have said to me, "But you don't understand. I have to work in a secular job around all sorts of worldly people."

I tell them, "Well, good for you. That is wonderful. You are to be salt in this world. (Matt. 5:13.) Salt flavors food. As you keep your thoughts and words in line with the Word, you will bring such an irresistible flavor to the world around you that people will want to savor whatever it is you have that's missing from their own lives. What an opportunity!"

Other people say, "But I can't continually meditate on the Word. It would interfere with my work."

You don't have to neglect your natural duties in life in order to meditate on the Word. This is especially true today since nearly everything under the sun has a Scripture on it—mugs, calendars, and screensavers for our computers.

If you don't do anything else, buy one of those daily calendars that has the date and a little "Scripture of the day" on each page; then meditate on that daily Scripture throughout the workday. Every time you look at the calendar as you sit at your desk and do your work, meditate on the Scripture. You do not have to use your brain to do that. You can keep the brain flowing with your work as you keep your spirit flowing with the Scripture. Your goal is to get that Word down into your spirit.

It is not that difficult to find a way to meditate on the Word. We make it hard with our natural minds, largely because we have been programmed by the world to respond to challenges with the words "I can't."

Those two words are not even in God's vocabulary. Instead, He gives us these words to confess: "I can do all things through Christ which strengtheneth me" (Phil. 4:13 KJV).

The only time God used the words "I can't" is when He said, "I cannot lie." (Titus 1:2.) Even then, He placed that restriction on Himself because of His own integrity.

So there are no "can'ts" in your walk with God, nor is there a good excuse for neglecting the Word. Meditating on the Word is the key that will cause you to become a light to this world. As you begin to speak forth the Word you have planted in your heart, you will become the creator of your own peaceful environment wherever you go and no matter what situation you face.

This is actually a good way to evaluate the status of your spiritual health. The best barometer you have is right under your nose. Every time you open your mouth, you have a choice to make. You can speak words that agree with God's Word and thus are full of life and power. (John 6:63.) Or you can speak words that agree with the devil's opinion, words that produce death, theft, and destruction. "The devil comes to kill, steal, and destroy" (John 10:10).

Ask yourself, *How is my barometer reading? Is my mouth speaking strife, or is it speaking kindness and blessing? Am I speaking words of death or of life?*

Any words you speak that are not in line with God's Word are not words of life. If you speak out of hurt and offense, or if your words reflect only what you think or feel, then you are speaking death and lies. Lies come from Satan.

Your mouth can set the atmosphere for the Holy Spirit to work mightily in your life.

Speaking God's Word is one way to fulfill the second guideline I want to share with you. After meditating on the Word, you have to practice the Word.

Too many Christians talk about how wonderful and how good the Word of God is. They love to hear the Word. The problem is, they never practice it.

Sure, these Christians know the Word of God, but it is meaningless if their knowledge is not doing themselves or anyone else good.

James 1:22 says, "But be doers of the Word [obey the message], and not merely listeners to it, betraying yourselves [into deception by reasoning contrary to the Truth]." We can meditate on the Word all day and night, every day of the week, but if we do not practice the Word we cannot walk in the fullness of the Holy Spirit. We will not know His voice when He speaks to us; therefore, we will not be able to walk in His perfect will for our lives.

You must be a doer of the Word and not merely a listener, for when you are just a listener, you are doing nothing less than betraying yourself. You are taking yourself into deception because you are reasoning with self rather than living according to the truth of God's Word. When you reason with self, you will get into trouble every time.

Let the Holy Spirit show you how to give action to God's will in your life. Whatever He reveals to you in the Word, remain determined to act on that truth in your daily life.

One important aspect of practicing the Word is to learn how to enter the presence of God. I am not talking about singing two or three songs on Sunday morning. For many Christians, that isn't a time set aside for entering God's presence in worship. Some of them actually think the praise and worship service is just filler to give the pastor time to get to church.

Certainly the praise and worship time at church is for your benefit, but you should come to church prepared to move into the presence of God. It should not take the praise and worship leader fifteen minutes to get you ready. Prepare yourself before you come to church by entering into praise and worship to the Lord on a daily basis.

The Holy Spirit will give you a new song every day as you avail yourself of Him. He desires for a fresh song of joy and peace to continually flow forth from your spirit. (Col. 3:16.)

And be not drunk with wine, wherein is excess; but be filled with the Spirit; Speaking to yourselves in psalms and hymns and spiritual songs, singing and making melody in your heart to the Lord; Giving thanks always for all things unto God and the Father in the name of our Lord Jesus Christ (Eph. 5:18-20 KJV).

However, the song of the Lord can only come as you stay in constant fellowship with Him—praising Him, worshiping Him, and loving Him more than anything else in this world. This is all part of practicing the Word of God.

Choose the Word First

The third guideline I want to share with you is that you must give the Word first place in your life. That means God is first before anything else. He is top priority in your life.

You can learn a lesson from the business world as you diligently pursue this goal. Business people are continually regrouping to evaluate their past and present performance and to make sure they stay in line with the goals and priorities they have established. As goals are accomplished, they then go back to reevaluate and set new goals.

It should be the same way in your relationship with God. Just because you have accomplished something He asked you to do in His Word, that does not mean you are finished.

Continue to return to God's Word so you can know you are setting new goals according to His will. Every time you do this, He will give you fresh understanding and wisdom to help you establish your new priorities and successfully fulfill the next step in your walk with Him.

One of my favorite passages of Scripture that talks about giving the Word first place is Proverbs 4:20-22:

> My son, attend to my words; consent and submit to my sayings. Let them not depart from your sight; keep them in the center of your heart. For they are life to those who find them, healing and health to all their flesh.

This passage says a mouthful. Every area of your life is covered right here because when you attend to His Word, you are submitting to His sayings. The only way you can submit to His sayings is to give them first place in your life.

God says you are to keep His sayings in the center of your heart and refuse to allow them to depart from your sight. You already know that you cannot walk around with the Bible in front of your face all the time. However, you can avail yourself continually of God's Word by speaking forth the Word that is already residing in your heart.

Words paint pictures. You must plant the Word on the inside of you by meditating on it and practicing it. Then as you speak it forth, you will actually begin to paint a picture of the manifestations of God's promises in your heart and mind.

You will be ready when you face a challenge or a difficult situation. The very first thing out of your mouth will be the Word—what God says about the situation and what He is going to do on your behalf as you stand strong in faith. That Word will paint a picture of your answer on the inside of you. And as you give the Word first place in your life, that answer will eventually be manifested in the natural realm as well.

Notice what God goes on to say in verse 23: "Keep and guard your heart with all vigilance and above all that you guard, for out of it flow the springs of life. Above everything that you guard in your life, you need to guard your heart."

Why does Proverbs 4:23 liken the heart to springs or waters of life? It is important to realize much of the Holy Land is arid and water is scarce. Without water humans, plants, and animals cannot exist. Water is life-giving and life-sustaining. It is an important symbol in the Bible. Just as plant, animal, and human life flows around an oasis or well in the desert, the heart is likened unto a water source from which spiritual life flows.

Proverbs 4:23 tells us all actions in life begin in the heart of the "inner" man. The condition of your heart determines whether you live wisely or foolishly. If you build your inner man on a foundation of the Word of God and prayer, you will live wisely. A foundation built on the world's opinions, values, and ethics produces foolishness.

The Hebrew word for "springs of life" can also be translated deliverance.[1] Again, because water delivers animals, plants, and humans from death in the desert. So you could say, "Keep your heart with all vigilance and above all that you guard, for out of it flows your deliverance." You can begin to see why it is so important to give God's Word first place in your life.

Most people would say you guard your heart by watching what you speak. You have to go back even further than that, all the way back to your thought life.

You have to guard your thoughts in order to guard your heart, because your mind is the real battlefield. Whenever you allow ungodly thoughts to take up residence in your mind, you are no longer guarding your heart. If you keep dwelling on those ungodly thoughts, you will soon be speaking out what you have been thinking—and therein lies the path to destruction.

So guard your heart with all diligence. Pay attention to the thoughts that run through your mind, and make a decision to think only on those things that are godly, virtuous, and true. As you speak forth those life-giving thoughts, you will keep deliverance continually working in your life.

Instantly Obey the Word

One more guideline for walking in the Spirit as a successful woman of God is this: You must learn to instantly obey the Word of God.

In Isaiah 1:19, it says, "If you are willing and obedient, you shall eat the good of the land." Many Christians are willing but not obedient. Many others are obedient, but they obey the Word only because they feel like they have to or because of what people will think if they do not.

If that is your motivation for obeying the Word, you are thinking carnally and you are *not* walking in the Spirit. Who cares what people think? If you are doing what is right, you are not worried about what people think, because your heart is pure before God.

However, it is not just a matter of being willing and obedient before God. You also have to learn how to instantly obey the voice of the Holy Spirit.

Once when I was studying this subject of obedience for the purpose of teaching on it, the Spirit of the Lord spoke strongly to my heart. This is what He told me: *You know, delayed obedience is not obedience.*

That hit me hard. Delayed obedience was one thing I knew I had been guilty of in the past. Procrastination is a problem that most of us deal with at one time or another. When God says, "I want you to do so-and-so," we respond by saying:

"Well, Lord, that isn't very easy,"

"I don't know if I can do that,"

"What is that person going to think of me?" or

"Maybe I'll do it tomorrow."

But tomorrow never comes because you begin to figure things out with your mental reasoning. You are not to reason with God when He tells you to do something. Your instant reaction should be, "When, Lord? Where? Who? How?"

The only way to grow into the woman God created you to be is to submit yourself to God and His Word. That is the beginning, not the end. You have to come to a place of total trust in God. You must know in your heart that you are pure before Him and that you are doing everything you know to do to follow His Word and to instantly obey His voice in every situation.

You will not always hit the mark. You are a human being, and you have to fight the carnal nature the same way everyone else does. Temptations and trials come to you just as they do to everyone else.

You may think it is easier for me to obey the Word because I am a minister. Although I stand up and teach the Word to people, I still experience trials and temptations.

The ability to obey the Word has nothing to do with whether or not you are a minister. The fact that you sit in the pew does not mean you are any less a woman of God than the woman minister who stands behind the pulpit. Your own neglect of your relationship with the Holy Spirit can make you less of a woman of God. Avail yourself of Him by getting in the Word of God and spending time in prayer, and then you can know for sure that He is working in every area of your life.

4

WALK IN THE LOVE OF GOD

The first thing God led me to study as a teacher of the Word was the subject of love. That is all I studied for two and a half years until Buddy and I began to pastor.

After we had become pastors of our first church, I teased our congregation and said, "Now I know why God led me to dig into the subject of God's love for so long."

The people understood that I was teasing. They knew I loved them dearly. The truth is, it was good that I studied the subject of love before I began to pastor. Just like everyone else in this world, I need to understand the love of God and be strong in my own love walk in order to work well with people in any arena of life.

The love of God involves speaking forth the truth in love to the people in your life even while loving them. You learn how to do that by practicing what the Word says about walking in the love of God.

The subject of walking in love has always been very important to me. I was raised in a minister's home, and I have been around Christians all my life. Over the years, though, I have seen Christians do many unloving things. God told me long ago, *I love people, and you're to love people as well.*

I responded, "Okay, God. You've taught me Your love, and I will walk in Your love. I love people. They may act ugly, but I will love them anyway."

If you are a parent, you know exactly what I mean when I say that no child always does everything you want him to do. At one time or another, every child acts ugly. You still love your children. You will always love them, for they are a part of you.

In a different but very real sense, the family of God is a part of you too. That's why the Word of God tells you to forgive rather than become offended, no matter what someone might do to you. If you hold on to that offense, you will not hurt anyone but yourself because you will begin to perceive everything in light of that offense rather than the way it really is.

There is just no getting around it. If you want God to work effectively in you and through you as a woman of God, you have to walk in His love.

I cannot stress enough the importance of walking in God's love. To me, the greatest love Scripture of all is John 3:16 KJV:

> For God so loved the world, that he gave his only begotten Son, that whosoever believeth in him should not perish, but have everlasting life.

God gave His best—His very own Son—so that we might be free.

This verse illustrates the manner of living God wants you to adopt for *your* life—the walk of divine love. He knows it is sometimes so easy to be caught up in your own little group, refusing to allow certain individuals into your life because they are unlovely or because they don't know God as you do.

When God gave His Son, not one of us was righteous. Nevertheless, God loved us enough to send His Son to die for us. That divine act of love allowed the living God to dwell within our newly created spirits.

You, too, are called to look at everyone through the eyes of unconditional love. As you let love mature within you, you will begin to reach out to others, even if they are unlovely. According to 1 Corinthians 13:8, God's kind of love never fails. As a result, you will find that people are drawn to you just because of your unconditional love.

God created man because He desired fellowship. Within every person, whether or not he or she is a new creation, is the desire to be loved and accepted.

However, the only way you can understand true love is by coming into an intimate knowledge of Jesus Christ and the Father God. In fact, when you study about love in the Word, you are actually seeking God Himself, for the Word says that God is love.

And we have known and believed the love that God hath to us. *God is love;* and he that dwelleth in love dwelleth in God, and God in him.

Herein is our love made perfect, that we may have boldness in the day of judgment: because as he is, so are we in this world (1 John 4:16,17 KJV).

When love is perfected in you, you don't try to obey what God tells you to do in the Word; you just automatically do it because God *is* love and when love is perfected in you, *God* is also perfected in you.

When God is perfected in you, you do not have to think about how He would react or what He would do or say in a particular situation. You just automatically act and talk like He does. Through Jesus you have been given that perfection in your spirit.

As we discussed earlier, Hebrews 11:6 says that without faith it is impossible to please God, but you also have to have the right motivation behind your faith. Your motivation should be love, the very essence of who God is. God *is* love, and He operates *by* faith as motivated by His love nature.

That is also how you are to operate in this life. Everything you do should be done because of the love of God rather than for selfish reasons. Selfishness is fleshly and carnal, and God operates only by the Spirit, never from the flesh.

The measure of your love is the measure of your worth to society. If you have been feeling like you are not worth much to society lately, check the measure of love you have been demon-strating in your life. Are you allowing love to flow from you as a mighty force to others in the measure God intended?

When you live with an understanding of your worth and the worth of others in the eyes of God, you will begin to influence those around you. Whether they are new creations or not, they will also begin to understand that they were created by God and have great worth in His eyes.

That is why it's so important that the love of God is perfected in full measure within you. Only then can you know how much you are worth to the kingdom of God and to society. Only then will you also see how much the people around you are worth as well.

Through the Word of God, you will begin to see people as God sees them. As you recognize an area of a person's life in which you can help, the compassion and the love of God will rise within you. You will find that you cannot just sit still and do nothing, for the divine love residing within will compel you to go forth and give of yourself.

Colossians 3:14 tells you what to do with the love of God:

> And above all these [put on] love and enfold yourselves with the bond of perfectness [which binds everything together completely in ideal harmony].

Before you can put on love, you must first receive Jesus as your Lord and Savior. At that moment, He and His Father come to abide within you through the Person of the Holy Spirit. (John 14:23.)

God is complete, and everything He does is complete. Therefore, as you allow His love to flow from you, that love begins to enfold you completely in a bond of maturity. This is a divine process that leads to a higher walk with God, where every relationship in your life is bound together in ideal harmony.

Be a Doer of Love

God created you to be a *doer,* not just a *hearer.* You have heard of the motto "practice makes perfect." That is a true statement. When you want to become good at something, you practice doing it repeatedly.

That is why God expects you to be a doer of the Word—it is the only way you will grow to maturity in the things of God. However, until you understand God's love, the other spiritual attributes that are supposed to abound in your life will never come to complete fruition.

God is love, and you are His child, a partaker of His very nature. Therefore, you, too, are love. The challenge you face is in allowing that love to work in you and flow through you in every area of your life.

A Christian who lives outside of love is destined for failure because she is living outside of God. Anything outside of God is not complete and will therefore fail.

Sometimes we see someone who is prospering and think, *She doesn't even know God, yet she's so successful. I knew her when she started in the mailroom. Now she's vice president of the company.*

Then we have a "pity party." We think, *I'm serving God. The Word says God prospers me in everything, but I can think of a lot of things I don't have.*

If that line of thinking sounds familiar to you, check yourself. If you are not abounding in love, you have found the reason you are experiencing lack in your life.

If you really knew that other person, you might find that she is unhappy, her home life is a disaster, her marriage is on the rocks, and her children are rebellious because they never had the attention and the love they needed to build character.

Those who live in spiritual darkness cannot understand love or allow it to flow in them. They understand only a natural, selfish love, which is based on performance. It is the kind of love that says, "If you will do this for me, I will love you. But if you won't, then forget it."

It is far better to come into the maturity of God's love and be successful according to the Word, than to be successful in the eyes of the world. The things you might gain on this earth are to no avail, but that which you gain in the spiritual realm will live on for eternity. That is far more important, for you are an eternal being.

So above all, be a doer of love. Let love be your primary pursuit in life. Love is the very nature of God, and God lives in you. Therefore, love is alive within you to help you fulfill everything God requires of you as a woman of God.

God has called you to go forth to help reconcile the world to Him. However, you can only fulfill that call if you allow love to be perfected in you. Otherwise, you will continue to limit yourself by looking at the world through your own eyes rather than through the eyes of love.

When you rely on what you can know about people in the natural, you will always be limited to that natural knowledge. On the other hand, divine love has no limits.

Therefore, you should confess this daily:

"Father, I thank You this day that You abide within me. Because You are love, I am love. I also thank You that the Greater One lives within me. Because You have overcome, I have overcome. Because You are more than a conqueror, so am I.

"I will never face a crisis alone, because You are always with me. You are there to make me a success by Your grace, which is Your great love in manifestation."

Whenever you fail to act in love, you can repent and say, "Father, forgive me"; then you can go on from there in His love. That is God's grace in manifestation.

In 2 Thessalonians 2:13 KJV, the apostle Paul gives guidelines that can help perfect you in your love walk toward other Christians:

But we are bound to give thanks always to God for you, brethren beloved of the Lord, because God hath from the beginning chosen you to salvation through sanctification of the Spirit and belief of the truth.

You are to thank God always for your brethren in the Lord. You are also to recognize that their faith is exceedingly growing, just as yours should be.

God wants His love to be abounding among the brethren until it gains absolute mastery in the church. That is the reason it is so important to be careful what you say about your brethren. If you speak negative words about someone, you are not walking in love. However, *you* will be the primary one hindered and hurt, not the one you are talking about. When love is not flowing, your faith is hindered—and as we have already seen, that means you are not pleasing God. (Heb. 11:6.)

If you are not walking in full faith toward God, you will not be looking at anyone else in faith. That means you will have problems trusting other people, including other Christians, because you have yet to learn how to trust God.

Let the Fruit of Righteousness Grow

If there is an area of your life in which you are experiencing a chronic problem, that tells you that in that particular area you haven't been working hard enough for fruit to be manifested on the vine.

A fruit tree in bloom is so beautiful. However, the time comes when the blossoms must fall off to allow room for the fruit to start growing on the branches.

In the same way, we look great and feel wonderful after coming into the knowledge of the saving grace of Jesus Christ. We want to tell everyone what God has done for us.

But there comes a time when the way we feel has to take second place to what God has told us to do. The fruit must begin to grow.

Just as a fruit tree has to be fed so its fruit can become plump and mature, you need to feed on God's Word so the fruits of righteousness can grow in your life. Negative circumstances will come, but you can eliminate their adverse effects from your life just as pesticides eliminate the bugs that infest fruit trees. Through your faith-filled confession of God's Word and your fervent prayers, you can take care of adverse circumstances.

Consequently, fruits of righteousness come into maturity in your life. People begin to say, "Every time I see you, you're always the same. You always have a glow about you. The love of Jesus is all over you." Comments like that let you know that the fruits of righteousness being perfected within you are showing up on the outside for all to see.

Now, remember that you often have to get close to a fruit tree in order to see the fruit growing on the branches. In the same way, you may not be able to clearly see the fruit growing in people's lives unless you relate to them on a day-to-day basis.

That makes it that much more important that you see your brethren in the Lord through the eyes of love, as Jesus sees them. You must believe that God is working in them and that their faith is growing exceedingly. This perspective allows the true love of God to flow freely through you to others, causing your own fruits of righteousness to come to maturity.

The first fruit that must grow in your life is love. The love that resides within you requires corresponding action.

The world looks at the natural circumstances. When people see no actions, they conclude that there is no love.

You have two responsibilities as a woman of God: (1) to demonstrate your love through actions so the world can see it, and (2) to endeavor to see your brethren as God sees them. As you are faithful to do these two things, you allow the full force of love to develop within you.

Confessing 1 Corinthians 13 every day will put action to the love within you. You will become aware of the love that is shed abroad in your heart as you hear and speak this passage of Scripture. It will become natural to live as love in action.

Personally, I continually confess, "God is love, and He is in me; therefore, *I* am love." Then I base the rest of my confession on *The Amplified Bible* version of 1 Corinthians 13:4-8. This is what I say:

"I endure long and am patient and kind. I am never envious, nor do I boil over with jealousy. I am not boastful or vainglorious, nor do I display myself haughtily. I am not conceited or inflated with pride.

"I am not rude and unmannerly, nor do I act unbecomingly, because I am love. I am not self-seeking; I do not insist on my own way. I am not touchy, fretful, or resentful. I take no account of the evil done to me, and I pay no attention to a suffered wrong. I rejoice not at injustice and unrighteousness but when right and truth prevail. I bear up under anything and everything that comes and am ever ready to believe the best of every person.

"My hopes are fadeless under all circumstances; I endure everything without weakening. I never fail, fade out, become obsolete, or come to an end."

God through Jesus has made you perfect; therefore, you, too, can say that your love will never come to an end. God says love never fails. Well, you are love, so you never have to fail in your love walk. God, an eternal being, made you an eternal being. You never fade out or become obsolete.

You have everything within you to make and to keep you perfect. Your body will one day decay and waste away, but the real you will live on forever—perfect and bound together in ideal harmony with God the Father.

It is important to let every fruit of righteousness become perfect unto full maturity within you. Just as you don't expect to see fruit the moment you plant a fruit tree, you can't expect yourself to bear full fruit overnight. God provides the direction you need to become perfected, but you must live His Word daily in order to see that fruit perfected.

Once you recognize all that is within you and the kind of woman God created you to be, you will say, "God's ability is within me, but now I must put it to work." You will realize that you were not put on this earth to be idle, allowing someone else to do your job. You are here to be ever busy—not pursuing your own selfish interests, but furthering the kingdom of God.

You can only work for God's kingdom in the fullness you desire by walking in the love of God. You are in God, and He is in you. His love in you demonstrated through action draws others into balance as well. Then they, too, can become complete in Him as they learn how to walk in the fullness of His love.

Perfected in Love

Whether you are young in age or young in the Lord, the following Scripture concerning love is a good one to help you grow in your love walk:

Let no one despise or think less of you because of your youth, but be an example (pattern) for the believers in speech, in conduct, in love, in faith, and in purity (1 Tim. 4:12).

Don't let anyone think less of you because of your youth, whether it is physical or spiritual. Don't retaliate according to what has been said or done to you either. Instead, let God's love work through you, and respond according to the Word. Respond according to the inward, not the outward, person.

One day when I was studying the subject of love, God said this to me: *When you dam up or hinder the love that wants to flow and express itself through you, the Word (Jesus) and My strength and power (the Holy Spirit) will not function properly through you, for they are both governed by love.*

Like a spring of pure, life-giving water, God's love needs to flow freely through you. If you carry your feelings on your shoulder and allow them to easily get hurt, you will dam up that spring spiritually. Soon you will be able to smell a stench.

Some people who dam up God's love cannot figure out why nothing works in their lives. They do not want to face the truth of the Word. They want the problem to be someone else's fault.

Don't make that mistake. If you have allowed God's love to be dammed up within you, let the Word begin to do a work in you. To stir up the love that the Holy Spirit has already shed abroad in your heart, combine praying in the Spirit with speaking the Word. As you do, love will begin to flow freely, washing away the impurities that need to go.

Think of how a river is formed. A small spring flows into a stream, which flows into a creek, which flows into a river. Nothing stops a forcefully flowing river. Anything in its way is washed along in its current. God's love will flow this same way inside of you once you ask His forgiveness and pull down the "dam" that has kept His love dormant and hidden within your heart.

In 1 Peter 4:8, God tells us to have much more than a casual, lukewarm love for one another:

> Above all things have intense and unfailing love for one another, for love covers a multitude of sins [forgives and disregards the offenses of others].

The *King James Version* translates the phrase "intense and unfailing" as the word *fervent,* which suggests the kind of white-hot flame required to melt pure gold. In other words, God is telling us to have such an intense, forceful love for each other that it binds us together in ideal harmony.

With your inner person full of God's Spirit and flowing with love, you are always ready to help and strengthen others. You are on the offensive—not the defensive—and nothing can stand in your way.

This is why you must keep God's love maturing within you by being quick to forgive, by living the Word, and by confessing daily who you are as a love person. You can also pray the following prayer in Philippians for others:

And this I pray: that your love may abound yet more and more and extend to its fullest development in knowledge and all keen insight [that your love may display itself in greater depth of acquaintance and more comprehensive discernment], so that you may surely learn to sense what is vital, and approve and prize what is excellent and of real value [recognizing the highest and the best, and distinguishing the moral differences], and that you may be untainted and pure and unerring and blameless [so that with hearts sincere and certain and unsullied, you may approach] the day of Christ [not stumbling nor causing others to stumble].

May you abound in and be filled with the fruits of righteousness (of right standing with God and right doing) which come through Jesus Christ, the Anointed

One), to the honor and praise of God [that His glory may be both manifested and recognized] (Phil. 1:9-11).

To develop to the fullest knowledge of love, you must love the Lord in the same way. Then as your love for others grows, God's glory will be manifested and recognized. That is why it is so important that you let the love of God mature in you and flow through you.

When the body of Christ as a whole comes into that fullness, a bond will form that cannot be broken. Everywhere we go, the glory of God will be manifested and recognized.

So make a quality decision to be diligent in your love walk. Discipline yourself to begin maturing in God's love. People will see Jesus in you and be drawn to the acceptance you show them through love. And the day will come when you walk in God's fullness as the loving, godly woman He created you to be.

Prophecy

You have heard it said in days gone by,
"How can I love? Look at my past
    and the things I have done."
But realize this, saith the Lord,
    I'm on the inside of you,
    and My love and ability flow out of you.

So learn to flow in My ability,
    saith the Lord,
    and learn to love with My love.

Lay aside the things of the natural.
Lay aside the things of the past,
   and realize that the God of the universe
   lives within you.

I am love, saith God,
   and I live in you.
My ability is in you today
   to reach out and love others.
So reach out in faith,
   and know that faith worketh by love.

My love is on the inside of you,
   so you can operate in My love
   and operate in faith,
   yes, even in the area of your home.
Yes, that one who sits
   by your side even now,
   love him in Me, saith God.

For I have given you the ability
   to love one another,
   and then the blessings of God
   shall flow in your place.
And, yes, there shall be a love atmosphere
   in that place.
You'll be able to say,
"It's because God lives within me.
We're operating in the God-kind of love,
   and it has totally changed our lives."

Others will say, "Teach us how
   to operate in that love."

And you will be a vessel used of Me,
   saith the Lord, because of My love
   flowing out of you—
My ability flowing out of you.
Listen to Me, saith the Lord.
You have it. You have it. You have it.
Now operate in it.

5

ABIDE IN THE PEACE OF GOD

Let's look at one more area in order to reach the fullness of God's plan for you as a woman of God. This vital key is learning to live in God's peace.

To walk in God's supernatural peace, you have to keep your mind tranquil and worry-free. It is easy for you to keep your spirit in peace because Jesus, the Prince of Peace, abides there. Your mind, however, is often another matter.

Jesus understands mental anguish because He identified completely with humanity and shared every aspect of human existence. (Heb. 2:14,15).

He was beaten.

He was ridiculed.

He was misunderstood, despised, rejected, and betrayed.

His family thought He was crazy.

His disciples deserted Him in His hour of need.

He suffered agonizing pain from a crown of thorns and crucifixion on a cross.

He was unjustly accused and classified a criminal.

Any one of those circumstances would cause mental anguish and emotional pain. Jesus experienced the greatest anguish and pain when He realized the Father in heaven had turned away from Him while He hung on the cross. "…My God, my God, why hast thou forsaken me?" (Matt. 27:46; Mark 15:34).

Just as a mentally deranged person doesn't look anything like he or she did before the breakdown, Jesus' face was unrecognizable. (Isa. 52:14.) He had been beaten. All the mental torment of the human race, the impact of alienation from God, and fear of death was placed on Him. (Heb. 2:14,15.)

Jesus suffered every mental attack you could ever come up against on that cross. He bore all that for you because He loves you so much. So when you feel like pulling your hair out from the mental stress of the problems you're facing, remember that Jesus already suffered for you, bearing the chastisement of your peace so you could have a tranquil heart and mind in every circumstance.

God wants you to take your place in the body of Christ. Sometimes it is easy to worry as you wonder, *What am I supposed to be doing? Where is my place?*

You will not have that kind of problem if you spend time daily with your heavenly Father and develop an intimate relationship with Him. You will become more aware of His peace,

His joy, and His love as you learn to hear His voice. Ministering daily to the Lord creates a strong desire in you to meditate on the Word.

When you read the Word aloud and hear yourself speaking it forth, you leave no room for unrest or disturbed thoughts. Nothing can penetrate the steadfast repetition of God's Word in your mind.

Sometimes when you fail to receive an immediate answer to your prayers, your mind can get out of peace. When that happens, your heart isn't the problem, because it is alive unto God. It automatically believes everything the Word says. The problem comes in your unrenewed mind—which, when left to itself, will follow the world's way of thinking.

Other times when you are standing in faith for what you have spoken, your mind begins to think back and wonder, *I don't know whether or not I did that right. Did I do everything I was supposed to do?* In that case, your mind only received by faith temporarily. When you allow your thoughts to bring everything back into the natural realm, you can keep the words you have spoken from happening.

That is why you must continually put the Word into your mind to keep it in agreement and at peace with your spirit. Then, when you speak forth God's Word, the answer will be manifested.

When the Lord wanted to create, He spoke what He believed. (Gen. 1.) His words brought life and transformed chaos into order. God believes everything He says with His whole being. Therefore, the moment He speaks something, it happens.

God created you to be like Him—spirit, soul, and body. He said we were made in His image. (Gen. 1:26.) When you believe with your whole being the Word that you have spoken, results to your prayers are manifested. If you are not experiencing results, the reason is usually that you are not completely at peace. You are trying to *make* the faith you have built within yourself work instead of *letting* it work.

You do not have to try to make your faith work. It is the God-kind of faith. God says your faith will work if you have renewed your mind and you believe His Word above everything else. When you are walking in peace and in the fullness of God, the words you speak forth automatically come to pass.

But it takes some effort to attain that place of supernatural peace in your mind. To that end, I recommend that you diligently meditate on this important passage of Scripture:

Jesus answered, If a person [really] loves Me, he will keep My word [obey My teaching]; and My Father will love him, and We will come to him and make Our home (abode, special dwelling place) with him.

Anyone who does not [really] love Me does not observe and obey My teaching. And the teaching which you hear and heed is not Mine, but [comes] from the Father Who sent Me.

I have told you these things while I am still with you. But the Comforter (Counselor, Helper, Intercessor, Advocate, Strengthener, Standby), the Holy Spirit, Whom the Father will send in My name [in My place, to represent Me and act on My behalf], He will teach you all things. And He will cause you to recall (will remind you of, bring to your remembrance) everything I have told you.

Peace I leave with you; My [own] peace I now give and bequeath to you. Not as the world gives do I give to you. Do not let your hearts be troubled, neither let them be afraid. [Stop allowing yourselves to be agitated and disturbed; and do not permit yourselves to be fearful and intimidated and cowardly and unsettled.] (John 14:23-27).

Jesus said, "Peace I leave with you." In essence, He was saying:

"My peace is all you need. I have told you My Father's sayings. You know His Word, and you know you are supposed to be doing that Word. Although I am going away, you will continue to know what to do because of God's Word.

"If you keep in your heart everything I have told you—if it becomes a part of you as you are faithful to act on it—the Holy Spirit, whom the Father is sending in My place, will bring all those things to your remembrance.

"Circumstances cannot take My peace from you unless you let them. So walk in My peace, for it is all you need."

Peace surpasses all understanding, and the world cannot take it away. Jesus made the point that if you neglect to renew your mind, you allow yourself to become agitated, cowardly, intimidated, disturbed, and unsettled. This can get you into trouble, for God is not the author of confusion. (1 Cor. 14:33.) When you get yourself in this dilemma, it is up to you to deal with the confusion and get back in the peace of God.

Some Christians continually want others to do the work and teachings of Jesus for them. These slothful people go from one meeting to another, getting spiritually fat but never acting on the Word. God once said to me, *This spiritual slothfulness grieves Me because it has delayed My coming.*

Other Christians overreact. They run around trying to do too many things for the Lord and, in the process, allow themselves to get agitated and disturbed. Finally they become worn out and ineffective—of little use to anyone, including themselves.

God has always desired that His people would march forth as a strong army. He wants every one of us to do the work He has called us to do as we walk in His supernatural peace. However, to live in the peace of God, we need to find the correct balance according to God's Word.

Stay in Peace

Years ago, the church where Buddy and I were the pastors was in the process of remodeling the north worship hall, and I was in charge of decorating. Buddy and I had to go out of town, so I left a list of things I wanted done, detailing when, where, and how.

When we returned home, it was time for Sunday services. I did not look at the progress on the north hall that day because I was there to minister to the people, but Monday morning I walked in and began to look.

The farther I walked down the hallway, the more agitated and irritated I became. Some items on the list either had not been done according to my instructions or had not been done at all.

As I reached the end of the hallway, I thought, *Satan, you're not going to rob me of my peace, because Isaiah 9:6 says that Jesus came as my Prince of Peace. Because Jesus abides within me, I have peace. According to John 14:27, Jesus said He left His peace with me, and the world cannot take it away. Therefore, Satan, you cannot take away my peace!* Then I began to pray in tongues.

Immediately God's peace rose on the inside of me from my spirit, where He lives. I calmly turned around and walked back down the hall to find out what had happened.

On my way, Satan tried to harass my mind with this thought: *You are a woman; the workers are men. You can't go up to them and say, "Why didn't you do this right?" They know what they're doing.*

I was walking in the peace of God, so I didn't let myself be intimidated by that thought. Although I might not have known how to do a particular thing, I knew what I wanted. After I had related to the men what I wanted, they should have done it according to my instructions.

Calmly, quietly, and in a spirit of God's love, I questioned the men. "Why was this wallpaper put here when it was supposed to be there? Why was this trim stained the wrong color? Why was this job not finished last week?"

The workers responded to my calm manner of speaking by apologizing; then they willingly worked with me to find an acceptable solution to the problem. This incident would not have ended so pleasantly if I had decided to react in agitation and anger rather than in the peace of God.

The same is true for you. If you determine to always respond to every situation in the love and the peace of God, you keep yourself from ever becoming disturbed, agitated, or intimidated. No matter what challenges or problems arise in life, you can walk through them all in the supernatural peace of God.

Prophecy

So don't be moved
    by the extraneous things that happen
    in your life.
Be moved by the faith that's on the inside,
    and rest in the peace it brings.

It makes no difference how things
    appear to be.
You know what My Word has to say.
You know what you have spoken.
And you know it has to conform
    and go that way.

So the peace and the rest of God
   should be that which guards
   your heart and your mind,
   keeping you from
   always reacting in agitation.
People who react to what's on the outside
   don't have My highest and best.
Peace doesn't react instantly;
It's always at rest.
It has acted beforehand
   on the Word that is true.
And if you will do that,
   peace will work for you.

When the telephone rings,
   don't panic; just say,
   "I'll be with you later.
   I'm going to spend time
   with my Father first."
Then the peace of God will keep you
   no matter what the news might be,
   because to make haste
   and react in the flesh is sin.
But to walk in faith and peace
   is good and right.
It will keep you in the right way.

So begin your day
   by walking in peace every day.

That way it will continue all day long.
Don't wait until the middle of the afternoon
    when everything begins to go wrong.
Start early, and continue therein.
Everything will work for good
    because the peace of God
    is keeping you as it should.

Part 2

❧

A Wife by Choice

6

A Godly Wife

We have talked about what it means for you to be a godly woman of God, functioning in the fullness of what God created you to be. This foundation must be strong and solid first if you are to learn how to be a godly wife in the eyes of God. As we discussed earlier, you are a woman by birth. You will discover how in the following chapters you are a wife by choice.

Again, Proverbs 18:22 says, "He who finds a [true] wife finds a good thing and obtains favor from the Lord."

A godly wife is a woman who knows who she is in God. God is first in her life. She understands her position as a wife and as a "helper meet" for her husband (Gen. 2:18), because she has a relationship with the Father God.

A "helper meet" is one who comes alongside her husband, making herself suitable, adaptable, and completing to him so he can become all God has called him to be. She is equipped to do so because she has already experienced spiritual fellowship and intimacy with the Creator. This helps her flow in the natural realm in her role as a suitable helper for her husband.

In order for you to become a helper meet for your husband, you must learn selflessness. You cannot fulfill your role as a suitable and adaptable helper to your husband while you are selfishly caught up with yourself and your own needs. As you put God's laws into action by fulfilling that role, you will also grow and become that which God has called *you* to be.

The second chapter of Genesis gives us important insight into God's original intent for woman as a helper meet. As you study this portion of Scripture, I believe you will be thrilled when you realize that God saw fit to create you a woman.

Then the Lord God formed man of the dust of the ground and breathed into his nostrils the breath or spirit of life, and man became a living being.

And the Lord God planted a garden toward the east, in Eden [delight]; and there He put the man whom He had formed (framed, constituted). And out of the ground the Lord God made to grow every tree that is pleasant to the sight or to be desired—good, (suitable, pleasant) for food; the tree of life also in the center of the garden, and the tree of the knowledge of [the difference between] good and evil and blessing and calamity.

And the Lord God took the man and put him in the Garden of Eden to tend and guard and keep it. And the Lord God commanded the man, saying, You may freely eat of every tree of the garden; but of the tree of the knowledge of good and evil and blessing and calamity you shall not eat, for in the day that you eat of it you shall surely die.

Now the Lord God said, It is not good (sufficient, satisfactory) that the man should be alone; I will make him a helper meet (suitable, adapted, complementary) for him (Gen. 2:7-9,15-18).

The Bible goes on to relate how God formed the animals and beasts and then allowed Adam to name them. God saw that Adam had no helper who was adaptable, suitable, and completing for *him*.

Genesis 2:21-25 tells us what God did about this problem:

And the Lord God caused a deep sleep to fall upon Adam; and while he slept, He took one of his ribs or a part of his side and closed up the [place with] flesh. And the rib or part of his side which the Lord God had taken from the man He built up and made into a woman, and He brought her to the man.

Then Adam said, This [creature] is now bone of my bones and flesh of my flesh; she shall be called Woman, because she was taken out of a man. Therefore a man shall leave his father and his mother and shall become united and cleave to his wife, and they shall become one flesh.

And the man and his wife were both naked and were not embarrassed or ashamed in each other's presence.

I want to lay a foundation so you can see some differences between man and woman. Genesis 2:7 tells us that God *formed* man. In the original Hebrew, one definition of being formed is "squeezed into shape."[1] The image is of a potter squeezing a clay jar into shape and depicts a man's close relationship to the earth.[2] That is probably why men often appear rugged.

In verse 22, we are told how God went about fashioning or building woman: "And the rib, which the Lord had taken from man, *made* he a woman, and brought her unto the man." The Hebrew word for made is *banah*.[3]

It seems to indicate that God paid even more attention to the creation of the woman than He did to the creation of man.[4] You could say that woman is more skillfully and carefully handcrafted than man because woman was made from man, not the earth.

The Lord showed me He used this manner of creation so a woman would be desired and admired by the man.

God created you to be more refined than a man is. That does not mean you are out of God's will if you are more athletic and not as dainty as other women you know. Do not compare yourself to other women. God made you the way you are, so accept it. If every woman were alike, this world would be rather dull. It would especially be hard on the men if women all looked and acted alike.

All women are different in aptitudes, in personalities, and in the things we like to do. Nevertheless, we are each skillfully and carefully handcrafted to be desired and admired by a special man.

Now let's look further at what God meant when He said this woman was to be a "helper meet" for her husband. The word *help* comes from a Hebrew root word meaning "to give aid and assistance" or "to surround in order to protect."[5] The word *meet* means "a counterpart" and comes from a root word that means "stand boldly out opposite."[6] You could say, then, that the woman was skillfully and carefully handcrafted to fulfill her role as the man's counterpart by continually surrounding him with aid and assistance.

You were created to be a helper meet as well. You were skillfully and carefully handcrafted to be suitable, adaptable, and completing to your husband. The way you fulfill that role is by continually surrounding him with aid and assistance.

Once you accept the role God has given you as a woman, you will be proud that your Creator created you a woman. He knew you could flow and walk in that role to perfection. He sees you as valuable and precious, and that is how you are to see yourself.

When you see yourself that way, it will make it much easier to see your mate the way God sees him. That is important. You were not made to help man see himself differently than the way God made him. You were created to make yourself adaptable, suitable, and completing for him.

What happens if you do not fulfill your God-ordained role as a helper meet for your husband? Well, you were created for man. Therefore, if you don't function in your marriage as you should—if you don't make yourself suitable, adaptable, and completing for your husband—you won't experience the sense of fulfillment that comes when you take your God-ordained place as his helper meet. That sense of fulfillment only comes when you do what God has called you to do as a wife.

You see, you are in a relationship with Jesus that parallels the relationship between a husband and wife. As a member of the body of Christ, you are part of the Bride, and Jesus is the Bridegroom. When you look to Him as your Source and go forth doing what He has placed you on this earth to do, you have close fellowship with Him and He meets your every need. But if you *don't* go forth in obedience to be His arms extended, you live with little sense of His presence. It becomes easier to forget that He is right there with you.

Genesis 2:24 KJV says that something wonderful happens when you do fulfill your role as a helper meet. "Therefore shall a man leave his father and his mother, and *shall cleave unto his wife:* and they shall be one flesh."

One meaning of the word *cleave* in the Hebrew is to never stop chasing or "to catch by pursuit."[7] In other words, if you continually surround your husband with aid and assistance, he will never stop chasing you. He will want you with him all the time because your presence in his life makes him complete.

God saw that man was not complete, so He created woman to be adaptable and completing to him. As you fulfill that role for *your* husband, your obedience to God causes your husband to be the same for you. You do not have to do everything, but you *are* accountable for your part.

Adapting to your husband is your role in helping him succeed. You allow him to be free to seek and to walk in God's will for his life. At the same time, your willingness to adapt yourself to your husband causes God's law of giving and receiving to go into effect on your behalf. You begin to receive everything you need and desire from your husband because you have become a great pleasure and delight to him.

Love never fails. When everything you do for your husband is done from a heart of love, he will respond to that love by giving in return. It works that way because love always draws a person to you; it never pushes away.

A marriage is not supposed to be one person giving and the other person taking all the time. There has to be a balance in the marriage relationship for it to work.

You were created for God first, and you first take pleasure in Him. Then you can also take pleasure in your husband because, as a woman, you were created for man. As you learn to take pleasure in the man God has given you, that brings him pleasure. As a result, pleasure is given back to you.

For some reason, vain thinking often blinds women. They begin to see themselves as indispensable assets in their husbands' lives. They think, *What would he do without me?*

Since you were created for your husband, not he for you, the real question is, *What would you do without him?*

You see, it isn't about what your husband can do for you, but what you can do for him. As you focus on blessing him, he will in turn be a blessing to you.

Another passage of Scripture that teaches this principle that woman was created for man says:

Neither was man created on account of or for the benefit of woman, but woman on account of and for the benefit of man. Therefore she should [be subject to his authority and should] have a covering on her head [as a token, a symbol, of her submission to authority, that she may show reverence as do] the angels [and not displease them].

Nevertheless, in [the plan of] the Lord and from His point of view woman is not apart from and independent of man, nor is man aloof from and independent of woman; for as woman was made from man, even so man is also born of woman; and all [whether male or female go forth] from God [as their Author] (1 Cor. 11:9-12).

Your husband was created to be the image and [reflected] glory of God (v. 7). This verse also says that woman is [the expression of] man's glory (majesty, preeminence).

You should honor your husband and respect the position God has placed him in. It is all a part of your adapting and becoming a suitable helper to him. As you fulfill your role as his wife, you cause him to be complete and to function fully on this earth as the man God has called him to be.

When God said a wife is to be adaptable, suitable, and completing to her husband, He meant in *every* area—spirit, soul, and body. But there is a necessary order to this process. Before a husband and wife can fulfill their scriptural roles in a marriage, they have to be joined in the Spirit first; only then can they successfully work on the soul and physical areas of their relationship.

These principles governing the marriage relationship are not something the world thought up. They come from God. If there are times in your marriage that you feel like you and your husband are being drawn away from one another, don't get your eyes on the circumstances or on your mate and say, "Well, the problem is that he does this and he does that. That's the reason we're having problems."

No, check yourself. Let the Lord show you the areas where you may not be fulfilling your responsibilities as you should. As you open your heart to the Lord and allow Him to change you, you open the way for God to work in your husband's heart so the marriage relationship can get back on track according to the Word.

Adaptable but Faithful to Who You Are in God

Just because a wife is to be adaptable to her husband does not mean she is supposed to let him run all over her and push her into a mold of how he thinks she should be. She is still responsible to be who *God* has called her to be. That is a difficult concept for many women to comprehend.

Have you ever noticed in a marriage that it is always easier for a woman to adapt than for a man to do so? God created women to be adaptable. When the wife is adaptable, she makes it easier for the husband to change and adapt as necessary. He does not do well at adapting unless the wife does so first because, again, woman was made for man.

Nevertheless, your call to be a helper meet for your husband was never meant to keep you from being the woman God has called you to be. Perhaps you have a career or you work outside the home. There is not anything wrong with that as long as it doesn't become your first priority. The key is in keeping your priorities straight as you seek to obey God and adapt to your husband.

I didn't say this is always easy. As I said before, things don't just happen in life the way you want them to. You have to work at achieving your desired goals, including your goals for your marriage. You have to dig in the Word of God and find out what God says about the subject. Then with the wisdom you receive from the Word, you can begin to do what is necessary to make your marriage exactly what God designed it to be.

When you know that your actions are according to the Word of God and that you are doing what God has called you to do in your marriage, you can walk in peace. That abiding peace comes from knowing you are following God.

The book of Proverbs has other things to say about what constitutes a "godly wife."

A virtuous and worthy wife [earnest and strong in character] is a crowning joy to her husband, but she who makes him ashamed is as rottenness in his bones (Prov. 12:4).

Let's look first at the phrase "a virtuous and worthy wife." Noah Webster lists the following as definitions for *virtuous:* "morally good; acting in conformity to the moral law; practicing the moral duties and abstaining from vice; chaste."[8] The word *worthy* can mean "possessing worth or excellence of qualities, virtuous, estimable, suitable."[9]

Therefore, a virtuous and worthy wife is a good woman of moral excellence. She is righteous and pure, honorable and admirable. She is suitable and safe for her husband.

The verse goes on to say that this virtuous and worthy wife is earnest and strong in character. What does that mean? *Earnest* means "studious, diligent, ardent in pursuit of an object, serious in pursuit."[10]

The word *strong* has many meanings. Some of which are "having a particular quality in a great degree, not easily overthrown or altered, or having a great force of mind."[11]

A wife who is a crowning joy to her husband has a purposeful intent to be the wife God intended her to be. She is serious about it. She is not just playing games; she does not have a casual attitude that says, "Oh, well, if it doesn't work out, I can always get a divorce." She has a moral force of character within her that keeps her standing steadfast in the midst of every situation.

This woman is intelligent. She is not a robot. She can think for herself. She has all the knowledge she needs to become the woman and the wife she is called to be. She is fully equipped to help her husband fulfill God's highest in *his* life.

It is this type of wife who is "a crowning joy" to her husband. *Strong's Concordance* says that the word *crown* comes from a root word meaning "to encircle for attack or for protection" or "to compass."[12] That means one of the main things you are able to do in your role as a crowning joy to your husband is encircle him with protection from the attacks of the enemy.

You can encompass your husband with protection. Praying the Word of God over your husband is one way you encompass him with protection. From Psalm 91 you can pray for his physical protection. You can pray Paul's prayers from Ephesians 1:15-23, Philippians 1:3-11, and Colossians 1:9-12 for his spiritual wisdom, understanding, and discernment.

Buddy and I were in our thirty-third year of ministry when Buddy went home to be with the Lord. During those thirty-three years, there always seemed to be some woman who thought my husband was so wonderful and who just knew she was supposed to be the one married to him. The Word of God says the marriage union is holy and not something to be taken lightly. (Heb. 13:4; Matt. 19:4-9; Mark 10:5-12.) Yet these women would try to make people believe they were spiritual and knew God.

There are times you have to encircle your husband to protect him from attack. You stand your ground. You certainly do not stand back and say, "Well, maybe that's God." You do not let any woman intrude into your marriage union and play havoc with your husband's feelings. You have a God-given right and a strong foundation of moral excellence already built within you to go on the attack and protect your marriage.

Now, that does not mean that you beat up the woman who is closing in on your husband. You go on the offensive, whether it is through prayer or through confronting that person with the truth of God's Word.

Personally, I have stood in front of a woman before and said, "I want to tell you something. I cannot help how you feel or what you thought God said to you—it is not God. Buddy is my husband. He has always been my husband. He always will be my husband—and that's final." Then I turned around and walked away.

That was an example of going on the offensive, and it was my God-given right to do so. I did not act ugly toward that woman, but I was very firm. I had to do it for the protection of my marriage.

In my study of this verse in Proverbs, I also went to the dictionary to get a better understanding of what the word *crown* means. I found that when it is used as a verb, *crown* could mean "to impart splendor and honor" or "to bring to a successful conclusion." Another word used in the definition of *crown* is the word *culminate*, which means "to reach the highest point" or "to bring to a climatic or decisive point."[13] Also, one dictionary meaning for the word *compass* is "to achieve, accomplish, and obtain."[14]

So if you are a virtuous and worthy wife, earnest and strong in character, you are also a thing of splendor and honor to him.

You cause him to come to a successful conclusion. You cause him to reach the highest decisive point. You cause him to achieve, accomplish, and obtain the perfect will of God in his life because you continually adapt and make yourself suitable to him, completing him and surrounding him with aid and assistance. This is when you are his crown and his joy.

Joy is an emotion that is evoked by a sense of well-being. When you take care of your husband, when you possess what he desires, he experiences great pleasure and delight, as well as a constant sense of well-being. You are helping him become all he was created to be, and it brings him joy.

As you become this definition of a godly wife found in Proverbs 12:4, you cause your husband to walk forth in fullness, feeling completed. Therefore, he can be a success. He does not have to think, *Well, my wife doesn't like this, and she doesn't want this. She says she can't do this, so I guess I can't do it either.*

These kinds of thoughts can so distract a man that he becomes ineffective at following God's perfect will. A husband with a virtuous and worthy wife is satisfied. He is complete. He is walking forth in that which God has called him to do, and his wife is right there beside him, helping him.

As Proverbs 31:23 says, "Her husband is known in the [city's] gates when he sits among the elders of the land." This woman has done her part to help her husband become complete and to reach the highest point of all God intended him to be.

As a virtuous and worthy wife, you have an awesome responsibility. But you can rest assured that God created you in such a way that you can fulfill that responsibility as you depend on His strength and His grace.

Equal in the Sight of God

As women, we too often take advantage of the common perception that we are "the weaker sex." We want to sit down and let our men wait on us—to put us on a pedestal because we are such "delicate" ladies.

From God's perspective, you and your husband are equal. Remember, He created you for man. You are strong. You are perfect in the Lord Jesus Christ. You are called to be suitable, adaptable, and completing to him, continually surrounding him with aid and assistance. As you fulfill that call, you become his crown and glory, his joy and delight, the only woman he desires.

Realize you should be so thankful that God created you as a woman. You can walk in that perfection. You can be a crowning joy to your husband because God is the One who makes you virtuous and worthy. Then you make yourself earnest and strong in character by meditating and feeding on His Word until it is a part of you.

You should keep this goal ever before you. As you become a virtuous and worthy wife, a sense of fulfillment will grow within you. You will have the pleasure of knowing that you are not only pleasing God but also the man God gave you as you walk diligently after God.

Proverbs 12:4 does not just define a godly wife in the eyes of the Lord. It also describes a woman who is *not* a godly wife: "She who makes him ashamed is as rottenness in his bones."

During my years in the ministry, I have seen many ministers' wives who fit that description. I feel grieved for women like this because no matter what God or man does for them, they are never happy. It is never enough. They can always find something wrong.

Many times these same women are seeking after houses and material possessions rather than seeking after God. They are trying to find happiness in the natural, but they will never find it there. In the meantime, they are making life unbearable for their husbands.

Remember, Proverbs 18:22 says, "He who finds a [true] wife finds a good thing and obtains favor from the Lord." This type of woman is *not* a godly wife; therefore, she is not a good thing, and she does not bring her husband the favor of the Lord. On the contrary, she is keeping her man from functioning completely in the will of God. Her husband is not following God; he is following along after her. His entire focus is on trying to make his wife happy in order to keep peace, instead of on obeying and pleasing God. As long as he does that, he cannot obtain God's favor and blessings.

Personally, I would never want to be caught in the position of this type of wife.

Here's another Scripture that provides a good contrast between a godly wife and one who is "rottenness in her husband's bones":

House and riches are the inheritance from fathers, but a wise, understanding, and prudent wife is from the Lord. Slothfulness casts one into a deep sleep, and the idle person shall suffer hunger (Prov. 19:14,15).

Verse 15 is a good description of the woman who is slothful in her responsibilities as a wife. She suffers lack and is never satisfied, because she has neither been wise nor prudent. She has sought after a natural inheritance of material things. Yet even when she obtains what she has pursued, she is still not happy.

This woman's words and actions have prevented her husband from being successful and obtaining God's highest for his life. Now to add insult to injury, she begins to put him down all the time. She laughs at him in front of people. She says, "Oh, he never can do anything right."

Soon the words of this woman's mouth have penetrated her so deeply that she loses all respect for her husband. As a result, he loses all respect for himself and becomes exactly what she has spoken—at least in her eyes. At this point, she has become as "rottenness in his bones."

A wife who does this has prevented her husband from reaching the highest point of achievement in his life. She chose not to change herself through the Word and the Spirit of God, and then she took it out on her husband. She caused him to be focused on her instead of God until the marriage eventually became a bad case of "scrambled eggs."

We cannot unscramble eggs, but God can. That kind of situation in a marriage may seem hopeless, but God could turn it all around if the wife would just make the decision to allow Him to work in her.

> It is better to dwell in a corner of the housetop [on the
> flat oriental roof, exposed to all kinds of weather] than in
> a house shared with a nagging, quarrelsome, and fault-
> finding woman (Prov. 21:9).

You cannot say it any plainer than that. God is telling the husband that he would be better off up on a flat rooftop—sitting in a corner all by himself, exposed to all kinds of weather—than to be inside his home with a nagging, quarrelsome, and faultfinding wife. At least he would be out of earshot of her mouth so he could keep his peace with God.

A wife like that keeps a man from staying clear and balanced in life. He starts losing perspective and becomes confused. He cannot hear God in the midst of all the negative words, and eventually he falls by the wayside. As a result, he does not succeed as God has intended him to.

In that case, the man's lack of success in life will be on his wife's shoulders, not on his. God told her in His Word what to do, but she chose to go her own way.

Do not ever allow yourself to get in that position. If in times past you have done any of the things I have just described, do not remain in that place of disobedience. Go before God and allow Him to work in you to change you into the godly wife He created you to be.

Make Your Home a Place of Peace

One of the biggest changes we as wives need to make is in our love walk toward our husbands. When it comes to our men, we sometimes have a tendency to act opposite to the way the love Scriptures tell us to act.

For instance, here's one thing women often get fretful and resentful about. They say, "Well, my husband is out there with the public all the time. He gets to do this. He gets to do that. When he comes home, he never wants to go anywhere or do anything."

Remember that you were made for your husband. It is up to you to make yourself adaptable to him. So try to understand his side. Realize that he has been out there all day long with people who have badgered him, pushed him, and put him down until all he wants to do is return to the home God has given him. And when he gets there, he wants it to be peaceful and full of joy.

That is *your* job. You can make your home a place of peace by accepting your role and doing your part as a godly wife according to the Word.

It is so important that you make your home a place of warmth, peace, joy, and love. Do everything you know to do to make your home something more than a place to hang your hat.

Today, it is so easy to reduce home to nothing more than a "weigh station" because it is such a busy world. There is always somewhere to go, someone to see, and something to do.

So it is up to you as a wife and mother to do whatever is necessary to make your house a happy, peaceful home, a place that is inviting not only to your husband and children, but to other people as well.

As my children were growing up, people were always visiting our home, whether they were my children's friends, my friends, missionaries, or ministers. That was fine with me. I have always enjoyed having visitors. I determined that no matter who was in my home, my home would always be a place of peace.

To this day, there is always peace in my house. God's peace never goes away or subsides in my home, because I continually call it forth by faith. My house is full of the glory of God because of my prayers and the prayers of others who have been in my home and prayed with me. I desire God's glory, so I maintain it in my home.

I have had people come to stay overnight at my home feeling very stressed. But after sleeping in my guestroom, they get up the next morning and say, "I can't tell you the last time I relaxed and slept so well. This house is so peaceful. There is so much of God here."

That is how your home should be as well. You need to make sure you take the time to maintain peace and order there.

Before I ever got my first dishwasher years ago, I remember how much I hated to leave home with the dishes still in the sink. I knew it was my responsibility to make sure everything was in its place in our home, but sometimes I just did not have time.

You may be thinking, *What difference does it make if everything is in its place all the time?* It makes a lot of difference. You see, clutter creates cluttered minds. I do not know about you, but I cannot function in clutter. Clutter causes confusion and makes it difficult to think of what you need to do to follow through on all your responsibilities.

So walk in love and understanding toward your husband, and concentrate on making your home a peaceful refuge for him to return to at the end of the day. No man likes to come home to a place that is full of chaos and unrest—and that should be true of you as well.

I have made several points in this chapter about what it means to be a godly wife. Many times when I begin to teach on this subject, women get sober. They do not like to hear it because they do not want that responsibility.

Whether you want it or not, you already have the responsibility to be a godly wife in the eyes of God. Therefore, you may as well learn to walk in that responsibility so you can reap the good results of it.

7

THE WIFE GOD
CREATED YOU TO BE

Marriage is a holy institution created by God Himself.
Within that divine institution, we have seen that woman was
created to be the expression of man's glory, majesty, and preeminence. (2 Cor. 11:7.)

This is the reason it is so important before you ever marry to
establish your relationship and fellowship with the Father God.
The intimacy you first experience with God will cause you to be
effective in your relationship and fellowship with the man He
gives you in marriage.

Every area will automatically fall in place as you learn exactly
how and why God created you and then begin to flow in your
divinely appointed role as a wife. It won't be something you
have to think about, wondering, *Now, is this right or is this
wrong?* You will know exactly what God says about the role you
are supposed to fill in your husband's life.

Most importantly of all, you will understand that your husband is not your source. God may use him to provide for your needs, but that man is not your source. *God* is.

It did not take me very long to learn that. People who knew Buddy and me in the latter years of our marriage assumed we had always been at the level we were at then. No, we had to grow in ability just as you do. We had to grow in our businesses, in our ministry—in all the things God had given us to do.

When Buddy and I first got married, we were both going to college, so finances were a little tight, but we thanked God for what we had. We understood the principles of the tithe, and we never had too little to pay tithes.

God is your Source. He is the One who will rebuke the devourer for you. He is the One who will open the windows of heaven and multiply your tithes back to you. All you have to do is be obedient to pay your tithes. He will do it because He said He would. It is that simple.

As Buddy and I grew in the Lord, so did our finances and everything else that pertained to us. The key lay in paying our tithes and in seeking God first. We both understood that He was our Source.

In Matthew 6:33, Jesus said that when you seek His kingdom, He will see to it that all things are added unto you. But your ability to enjoy the "all things" promised to you is directly connected to your learning the voice of the Holy Spirit. That's the only way you can know on a daily basis that you are following what God would have you do for that day.

Through your close relationship with the Lord, you learn that submission is an attitude of the heart, not a physical action. As you learn to submit yourself to Him, it becomes easier for you to submit yourself to your husband as unto the Lord. (Eph. 5:22.)

Once you have truly learned how to submit to Jesus in love, you have no problem submitting to your husband in love. That doesn't mean you are a robot who does your husband's bidding without a thought of your own; you are submitting to him as a voluntary choice of the heart. As you do, both you and your mate will bring balance to each other as you grow into the complete union of one flesh that God desires of you.

Of course, submitting to your husband does not mean you are there for him to push around. It does not work that way.

I related to you earlier how God changed me from a shy and easily intimidated person to a bold person completely free from fear. When I came out on the other side of that struggle, my husband used to say to me, "Man, you're about as strong now as three acres of garlic!"

Buddy said that because I was different than I was before. Instead of always hedging around what I really thought, I now stood up and spoke it out. I had learned that it is important to know who I am and to recognize who God has called me to be, not only in the ministry, but in my marriage as well.

Buddy and I had a good relationship. I looked for things to do for him, and he did the same for me. Our hearts were to serve each other, yet we were not one another's servant. Neither of us took advantage of the other's desire to give and to serve.

You have to learn to set these boundaries within your own marriage as well. Once again, let me stress that you must understand who you are in God. This helps you set correct boundaries according to the Word as you willingly submit to your husband.

When the Husband Is Not Living by the Word

First Peter 3 gives some important guidelines for wives regarding this subject of submitting to husbands—even husbands who are not living according to the Word.

In like manner, you married women, be submissive to your own husbands [subordinate yourselves as being secondary to and dependent on them, and adapt yourselves to them], so that even if any do not obey the Word [of God], they may be won over not by discussion but by the [godly] lives of their wives, when they observe the pure and modest way in which you conduct yourselves, together with your reverence [for your husband; you are to feel for him all that reverence includes: to respect, defer to, revere him—to honor, esteem, appreciate, prize and, in the human sense, to adore him, that is, to admire, praise, be devoted to, deeply love, and enjoy your husband].

Let not yours be the [merely] external adorning with [elaborate] interweaving and knotting of the hair, the wearing of jewelry, or changes of clothes; but let it be the inward adorning and beauty of the hidden person of the heart, with the incorruptible and unfading charm of a gentle and peaceful spirit, which [is not anxious or wrought up, but] is very precious in the sight of God.

For it was thus that the pious women of old who hoped in God were [accustomed] to beautify themselves and were submissive to their husbands [adapting themselves to them as themselves secondary and dependent upon them].

It was thus that Sarah obeyed Abraham [following his guidance and acknowledging his headship over her by] calling him lord (master, leader, authority). And you are now her true daughters if you do right and let nothing terrify you [not giving way to hysterical fears or letting anxieties unnerve you] (1 Pet. 3:1-6).

Let's start with the first verse. If your husband is not living according to the Word, you are to win him over, not by discussion, but by your godly life.

You should be very careful not to present yourself to your husband as having greater knowledge than he does.

This can be especially difficult if you have come into the knowledge of God's Word and have received the Holy Spirit but your husband is not at that point yet. Revelation knowledge starts coming strong and fast into your heart. The desire within you to grow in the Lord gets stronger and stronger.

That is fine. But remember it is your responsibility to encircle your husband and protect him from attack. If you get so taken up with your own growth in the Lord that you can only think of yourself, you have left the realm of protecting your husband and have moved into the realm of selfishness. You are no longer keeping him from the enemy's attacks.

You surround your husband with protection by your manner of living and by how you treat him. Even if you are born again and he is not, that does not change your marriage relationship. It should only place within you a stronger desire to love him and to surround him with prayer and the God-kind of love. Your husband will then recognize that, although something big has changed in your life, it has not changed your relationship with him. You still love him, respect him, and submit to his leadership in the home.

If you do not think you can do that, the love of God is not operating in you. The Bible says God so loved the world that He gave His only Son. (John 3:16.) God gave the best He had. He accepted us all just as we were in our unlovely state. If you are like Him, you have to do the same for your husband.

You must accept your husband as he is, knowing that as you reach out to him in the pure love of God, you will draw him both to God and to you. Your godly manner of living will eventually cause him to come into the blessings of God you have learned to enjoy.

Do not allow yourself to adopt a superior attitude over your husband. Although you may be Spirit-filled and are gaining a fuller knowledge of the Word, that does not make you any better than the man who is your mate. If you loved him before you came into this greater spiritual knowledge, you had better love him just as much after you have come into it. In fact, the love of God should be so predominant within you that you treat him better than you ever have before.

It is true that sometimes our husbands have characteristics that we do not like and do not want to put up with. But because of the love of God within us, we *must* put up with those unpleasant qualities in order to win them over to the Lord.

I know. I have been there. Buddy and I were very young when we got married. He knew the Lord, but he had never been taught the Word and had become very disillusioned.

In our early years of marriage, Buddy was very carnal. Although I knew how to pray, was brought up in a Christian home, and knew more of the Word than my husband did, that didn't mean I was without my own set of faults.

We tend to look at our husbands' faults instead of our own when we know they are not in fellowship with God as they should be. We perceive them as being in worse shape than we are.

If you will just keep working on yourself, continue to pray and do what you know to do as the woman God has given your husband, you will win him over faster and sooner than you ever could by preaching at him.

Your husband will see that you have not changed as far as your natural responsibilities are concerned. You still get up and cook his breakfast. You still get him off to work. You still clean the house. You still take care of the home as you always did, because taking care of your family is still your top priority.

When you keep God's perspective regarding your responsibilities to your husband and your home, God always makes sure you have the time you desire and need for Him. On the other hand, if you try to grab the time on your own terms, you'll create problems in your home and in your marriage.

Some women are all caught up in a frenzy of going from meeting to meeting. They say, "Oh, I just have to learn more about God. There is a Bible study here Monday night and a 'bless-me service' over there on Tuesday night. Wednesday night is my church's regular midweek service. Then on Thursday night, so-and-so is in town, and I just have to hear him preach. On Friday night, a weeklong seminar starts."

These ladies are going somewhere every night in the name of God, and then they wonder why their husbands get angry with them and the Lord. The reason is that they are not fulfilling their scriptural role as wives. Instead, they have taken on the role of spiritual hobos.

The Bible does not tell us that we are to run here and there and do this and that when we begin to walk in God's fullness. Just like the virtuous wife of Proverbs 31, we are to be diligent and faithful to fulfill our responsibilities to our families. There will still be time to grow in our knowledge of God and His Word. If we allow God to guide us, our spiritual growth will never be gained at the expense of our families.

How To Treat Your Husband

First Peter 3:2 goes on to tell us which qualities should be included in our "godly manner of living." Notice how this verse starts out: "When they [your husbands] observe the pure and modest way in which you conduct yourselves...."

Are you conducting yourself in a pure and modest way in the eyes of your husband? You may not have thought about this question before. Because of my position in the ministry, I often see this verse inadvertently violated in Christian circles.

I'm talking about women who get turned on to the Word of God and to the fullness of the Holy Spirit and then start letting the love of God flow when fellowshipping with other believers. These women hug both sisters and brothers in the Lord without even thinking about how it might be perceived by their husbands.

Be careful about doing that, especially if your husband is not a Christian. He will not understand why you are doing that. He still thinks as the world thinks. Immediately the devil will come to his mind and say, *The reason your wife likes the church so well is that they practice all this free love. She can go around and hug all these men, all in the name of Jesus.*

Conduct yourself modestly with other men, including your Christian brothers. Remember that you have the ability to win your husband as he observes your modest and pure manner of living.

That does not mean you have to put yourself in bondage, but be very careful. Keep yourself in the presence of the Lord at all times. He will help you act in wisdom according to His Word.

Your husband will be won over as you continue to reverence him:

> When they observe the pure and modest way in which
> you conduct yourselves, together with your reverence [for
> your husband; you are to feel for him all that reverence
> includes: to respect, defer to, revere him—to honor,
> esteem, appreciate, prize and, in the human sense, to adore
> him, that is, to admire, praise, be devoted to, deeply love,
> and enjoy your husband] (1 Pet. 3:2).

Your husband may not be living according to the Word, but
he is still your husband. No matter what kind of spiritual
change you have experienced, that does not change your marriage relationship. In fact, because you have found the truth,
you should reverence, honor, respect, and defer to him even
more than you did before.

This is where many women are hung up in their preconcep-
tions of what it means to reverence their husbands. They say,
"How can I defer to my husband when I know his decision
isn't right?"

Have you determined that your husband is wrong because
you think he is not as mature in the Lord as you are and therefore does not understand as much as you do? On the other
hand, does his decision go against the conviction you have in
your heart through your close fellowship with the Father God?
There is a fine line here, and it's up to you to find out which side
of the line you're standing on. It's a big responsibility.

Reverencing your husband also includes adoring him. In times past when I would say, "I adore my husband," some women would reply, "But you're only supposed to adore God."

"No," I'd answer, "the Bible tells me differently in 1 Peter 3:2." Just as in the spiritual sense you are to adore God and give Him first place in your life, in the human sense you are to adore your husband and give him first place in your heart over any other human being. It is your place as his wife to praise him, respect him, and be devoted to him. As you do that, you allow the love for him that is already in your heart to grow deeper and deeper. This love enables you to fully enjoy and take pleasure in your husband the way God intends.

Pray for Your Husband

One of the most important things you can ever do for your husband is pray for him on a daily basis. Here is an example of what I mean:

"Father, I thank You that Your life is within my husband and that he will flow in Your will this day. He will see the people around him who are in need and will know what to do to reach out and help them. He will be able to turn his back on those who jeer at him and give him problems, and then walk on in success. He will speak forth the words You desire him to speak. He will not give in to the flesh or retaliate if people treat him wrong or speak against him in any way."

After you have prayed everything you know to pray in English for your husband, begin to pray in the Spirit for him.

Let your spirit soar up into the realm of the Spirit, knowing that you are praying the perfect prayer for him because you are standing in the gap for him. Anything that tries to come against him that day will not penetrate.

This is the way you become effectual in helping your husband attain the fullness of God's plan for his life. Remember, you were made for him. As you are faithful to pray for your mate, you will see mighty things take place both in his life personally and in your union with him.

A wife is called to no greater ministry on this earth than to pray for and to minister to her husband in the ways I've been describing. Yet in this day and age, the big thing with many women seems to be "my ministry."

We all have a ministry. God says we are all here to reach out to people with the ministry of reconciliation. (2 Cor. 5:20.)

Even if God has placed a more specific call to the ministry on your life, you must realize that the Bible plainly says that God instituted the home before He did the church. If there were no homes, there would not even be a need for churches. Therefore, as I said before, if you are putting your ministry before your husband and your children, you are out of the will of God and playing into the hands of the devil.

You see, the enemy wants you to neglect your family in favor of your ministry. He likes to use that error to find an open door into the home. Then he divides and separates the family members in an effort to make the family unit fall apart. He knows if he can get enough families to fail, there won't even be a strong, united church for him to deal with.

I remember a woman who fit this category I am talking about. I learned about her when I spoke at a certain ladies' luncheon at a regional convention.

I did not know any of the women attending that luncheon. I just spoke according to what God had led me to share with them.

This lady was in charge of taking up the offering. I did not know her position or anything else about her.

When it was time for me to speak, I got up and began to talk about a woman's responsibility to put her family before her ministry. This woman sat on the front row, so it was easy for me to observe her response to what I was saying. Until then, she had been friendly and all smiles. As I continued to speak, I saw a big frown replace the smile on her face, and I thought, *What did I say to make her mad?*

When I encounter that kind of opposition, I usually overlook it and go on because I know people are not offended because of me, but because of the Word. Later, a friend of mine visiting from another state came over to me and asked, "Did you see the way so-and-so responded to your message?"

I asked, "Who is that?" The name did not even register with me.

My friend answered, "The lady who took up the offering."

"Oh, yes, I know who you're talking about. I noticed that something I said made her angry, but I was so involved in teaching the message, I couldn't figure out what I said that offended her."

My friend explained that this woman had come out of the bondage of an extreme doctrinal teaching about the role of women. According to this teaching, women could not even speak unless they were spoken to.

Because the woman had been in this type of bondage for so long, she didn't handle her new freedom well and went straight into the ditch on the other side. She became so involved in ministry that she did not have time for her husband. She did not have time for her children. She did not have time for her housework.

My friend was staying in this woman's home during the convention and said she had never been so shocked in her life as she was when she entered the woman's home. Unwashed dishes, dirty clothes, and piles of junk were scattered everywhere. My friend also said that the woman ran into the house just before it was time to go to the meeting and said to her husband, "I'm sorry, you'll have to take the kids out and buy them some lunch. We have to go."

My friend told me, "It's been that way ever since I've been here. She has not cooked one meal. The children are fed only when the husband takes them out to eat. If anything is washed, the husband is the one who does it. She doesn't have time because she has a ministry."

That is not the will of God. That is not functioning in the position God created a woman to fill.

Live Your Life in the Order of God

Don't take this point lightly. If you know you are called to the ministry and are busy working for God, that is very good—but it cannot be your first priority.

You may protest, "But I thought I was created for God first."

It does not say in Genesis that you were created for God for the sake of ministry. It says you were created for God for the sake of fellowship. He desires an intimate relationship with you, one in which you adore Him and find the time to walk and talk with Him just as Adam and Eve did.

In that sense, you were first made for God. Right after that, you were made for man. When you are in right relationship with God, you will know that you are to put your husband first in your life before any ministry you are called to fulfill.

Do not put your children above your husband. That has caused many divorces for so many couples later in life.

Let me explain the way it often happens. When the children come along, the husband gets busy making a living and the mother gets busy raising the children. She makes sure the children have everything they want. She helps them get involved in every possible activity that will make them look important in the eyes of others.

Then when the kids grow up and leave home, Mom and Dad do not even know each other anymore because they have gone their separate ways. The wife has lost interest in her husband because she has spent years pouring all her energy and love into her children.

God did not create you for your children. There would not even be any children if it were not for your union with your husband in the first place.

God made you for man. The children are strictly a pleasure and a blessing resulting from the union of you and your husband as one flesh. Your children are in your life for you to bring up in the knowledge of God's Word. Then they, too, can grow up to function fully in their roles as godly men or women, just as God created them to function.

God enables you to first become one in spirit with a man and then to become one in soul and body. Consequently, you reap the benefit of beautiful children. This is your privilege as a wife. If you properly teach those children the Word and live a godly example before them, they will be a pleasure to you. But if you put your children before your husband, you will reap a negative harvest, and every family member will ultimately suffer for it.

Putting your children before your husband will push him away from you. It will cause a breach in the spirit, and the Bible says, "...Thy breach is great like the sea: who can heal thee?" (Lam. 2:13 KJV). That breach will get larger and larger until it becomes so large that you and your husband are no longer one in spirit.

Eventually, your husband will find other interests to fill the void. Then when your children have gone on to live their own lives, you will be left with an all-too-common situation of two people who don't even know one another living in the same house. And because it has been that way for so many years, neither one of you may even have the desire to be acquainted all over again. You may prefer to just keep going your own separate ways.

That is not a description of a home. It is nothing more than a house. And if you do not do something about the situation, you may end up finalizing the separation that already defines your marriage. That is not God's best.

Put your husband before your ministry or work. Put your husband before your children and put God first. It is that simple. Live your life in the order of God and in line with the Word. You will reap great benefits as you become the wife God created you to be.

8

BIBLICAL GUIDELINES FOR THE MARITAL RELATIONSHIP

The Bible is very clear in providing a picture of the marriage relationship as God designed it to be. If we wanted to describe that scriptural picture with only one thought, we might say, "A husband and wife are to take pleasure in each other." Each marriage partner is to be a delight to the other—spirit, soul, and body.

Let's go back to 1 Peter 3:2 for a moment. We saw that one aspect of reverencing your husband is to enjoy him. The dictionary definition of that word *enjoy* is "to take pleasure and satisfaction in; to have for one's use or benefit."[1]

You are to take pleasure in him and have satisfaction in him. He is not in your life for you to maneuver, manipulate, and take advantage of. He is there so you can enjoy the great benefits of loving him.

In light of this truth, I first want to focus on what the Bible says about your physical relationship with your husband. An important passage of Scripture along this line is in 1 Corinthians 7:

> For the wife does not have [exclusive] authority and control over her own body, but the husband [has his rights]: likewise also the husband does not have [exclusive] authority and control over his body, but the wife [has her rights].

> Do not refuse and deprive and defraud each other [of your due marital rights], except perhaps by mutual consent for a time, so that you may devote yourselves unhindered to prayer. But afterwards resume marital relations, lest Satan tempt you [to sin] through your lack of restraint of sexual desire (1 Cor. 7:4,5).

Paul is saying that neither you nor your husband has full authority and control of your own bodies. You are each to give freely of your body one to the other because you have become one spirit, soul, *and* body.

That means you should treat his body as your own, and he should treat your body as his own, never abusing or taking advantage of or drawing away from each other physically.

God commands you as a wife never to refuse, deprive, or defraud your husband of his marital rights in the sexual realm. If this is difficult for you to accept, I want you to understand that man-made religion and tradition are influencing your thinking, not the Bible.

You are to *enjoy* your husband, and he is to enjoy you. You are to take pleasure and find your satisfaction in each other. He is for your use and your benefit, and you are for his use and his benefit. You need to learn this principle, especially in the realm of your sexual relationship.

Over the years as I have counseled married couples, this is the area in which many of them had problems. Nine times out of ten, I found that the woman was too cold. She did not enjoy herself in her sexual relations with her husband. This caused tension in her husband because he felt as if he was unable to satisfy her. Therefore, he had drawn away from her.

In the generation before mine, sex was considered a dirty word. Religion dictated that decent people did not even mention that word in public conversation. Christians were looking at Satan's perversion of sex and not at the blessing God originally created it to be between husband and wife.

Your sexual relationship with your husband is the gift God gave both of you to cause you to become one flesh and to be fulfilled together physically. It would behoove you to study this subject in the Scriptures and find out exactly what you are supposed to do.

I've had women say to me, "Well, I just can't give vent to how I feel when I'm making love to my husband. I would be so embarrassed."

Why should you be embarrassed? You and your husband are one flesh. He desires you to give vent to your feelings at that time so he can know that you enjoy him as much as he enjoys you. And as you give of yourself fully and completely to him in the physical act of love, not only will he be completely fulfilled and satisfied, but you will be as well.

There are many frustrated women running around, especially in religious circles. They do not understand why they are frustrated. They do not know that their problem lies in not allowing the true love of God to flow through them in their sexual relations with their husbands.

You cannot use the headache as your standard excuse. I am sure you will forget all about your headache once you start giving of yourself to your husband the way God intends for you to do.

You may be thinking, *Oh, my! She's being so crude.* Well, if I am being crude by saying these things, then so is God, because this is exactly what He says in His Word.

If you are having problems in this area, you need to get before the Father God and let Him show you what you are to do and how you are to respond to your husband. Keep in mind that 1 Corinthians 7 says the only time you are to withdraw physically from one another is for the benefit of devoting yourself to prayer without any hindrance. However, even then it is only to be done by mutual agreement. If you separate yourself physically from your husband without his agreement for the purpose of prayer, you're still not in obedience to the Word in this matter.

When God made you a woman, He skillfully and carefully handcrafted you to be desired and admired by your husband. Therefore, it is important that you fulfill that desire in the natural. If you do not—especially if your husband is not strong in the Word—you open the door for the lust of the flesh to take over. And if your husband starts looking at other women, it will be your responsibility.

Sexual relations are to our marriages what food is to our bodies. In the natural sense, without food you will die. Similarly, if a married couple does not have a healthy sexual relationship, then in that area of their marriage, death comes.

Death to a couple's sexual relationship doesn't come all at once, any more than death comes on the first day a person stops eating food. First, the couple must go through the tormenting process of slow "starvation." Finally, they reach the point where all feelings of sexual desire for each other have disappeared. That is when death has come to that area of their relationship.

If this should ever happen in your marriage, your spiritual life will become hindered until you make things right. You cannot enjoy intimate fellowship with God if you are not walking in His full will regarding your role as a wife.

I know this subject is rather heavy, but we need to think about it, especially in this day and age we are living in. Sex has become a household word in the eyes of the world. Years ago, sex was something people did not talk about. Now it is *all* people talk about. In fact, people often flaunt their openness about sex, and it is usually in the perverted sense.

You have to get beyond the way the world looks at sex and begin to see it as something pure, wonderful, and holy before the Lord. That is what it is to Him. He created sex to be a beautiful union between husband and wife, and you should look at it the same way. Sex is not something you just have to endure, like cleaning the house or going to the grocery store. No. Your sexual relationship with your husband is a vital part of the life-giving process God has provided to keep your marriage vital and strong.

Do not neglect this area of your relationship with your husband. It is so important for the health of your marriage that you work on becoming the wife God created you to be in the sexual realm.

As you do this, rest assured that He has given you every quality you need to make yourself suitable, adaptable, and completing to your husband. Just let those qualities come forth and flow from you to your husband as you take pleasure in one another physically. Soon you'll find that your sexual relationship with your husband has become a precious time in which you experience together the complete union of two lives—spiritually, emotionally, and physically.

Consecrated by Your Union

First Corinthians 7:14 explains further your responsibilities as a wife in your marriage relationship:

> For the unbelieving husband is set apart (separated, withdrawn from heathen contamination, and affiliated

with the Christian people) by union with his consecrated (set-apart) wife....

This is another reason it is so important to keep your union with your husband perfect and pure. If he is not living according to the Word, you are the one who keeps him separate from heathen contamination and affiliated with Christian people.

Verse 14 goes on to say this:

...and the unbelieving wife is set apart and separated through union with her consecrated husband. Otherwise your children would be unclean (unblessed heathen, outside the Christian covenant), but as it is they are prepared for God [pure and clean].

Thus, your children are protected and blessed—clean, pure, and prepared for God.

Your sexual relationship with your husband is only one aspect of your natural responsibilities as a wife. Some of your other natural responsibilities include keeping his clothes clean, keeping the house clean, cooking meals, and so forth. Willingly helping your husband in all these ways is a part of being adaptable and completing to him.

Another important aspect of the marriage relationship is the soul realm, which is made up of your mind, your emotions, and your will. You are to be adaptable and completing to your husband in this realm of your marriage relationship as well.

The best way we can do this is by developing our communication with our husbands. Communication feeds our thinking faculties, and that affects our emotions. If we communicate properly, we prevent the enemy from bringing thoughts into our minds that cause us to waver in our marriage relationships. There will not be any room for wrong assumptions in the mind that say, "I really don't know him as I should."

It may seem to you that you can talk more freely to a friend than to your husband. Your husband should first be your friend and then your lover. You must learn to communicate well with him, sharing your innermost thoughts and feelings, so your friendship can grow and your union can be complete.

For instance, you might share with your husband what God showed you in your devotions that day. Then the truths you have learned that ministered most to your heart will also minister to him. Also, share with him your feelings. Communicate with him about everything you are involved in.

Now, that doesn't mean you're supposed to meet him at the door and say, "Oh, my God! You do not know what happened to me today. You just will not believe it. I hardly coped with it." That is not communication. That is venting your frustrations all over your husband.

Buddy and I always shared the Word together, although we were often studying different subjects. Something I would share with him often triggered a revelation within him, bringing light to the subject he was studying. The same thing would happen when he shared a scriptural truth with me. These times of sharing the Word together helped us keep a balance spiritually both in our personal lives and in our marriage.

Buddy and I also spent a lot of time communicating our thoughts and feelings with each other. We came to know each other *very* well. I knew exactly how he would act or react to situations. I knew what he would do, what he would not do, what he expected, and what did not matter to him. In the same way, he knew all about me. Over the years, the intimacy that developed between us built a strong foundation of trust in our marriage relationship. We were true friends.

Too many times Christians are so caught up "in faith" that they think they cannot talk about their feelings because that would be confessing the wrong thing. If the feelings are already there, they are fact. That is just the way it is.

Now, it is a different matter when a wrong thought comes to your mind that you recognize and deal with. If you replace that negative thought with the Word before you ever speak it out, you never give it the opportunity to become a feeling. But when you have allowed Satan's attacks to come against you until strong feelings have become a part of you, you'd better talk about it with your husband.

This will help him understand you better. You can then join yourselves together in prayer and ask God for the wisdom to do something about the problem. Communicate these feelings and listen to your husband's responses. It may help you see ways in which the enemy has tripped you up and deceived you.

As you work on your communication skills with your husband, it is important to realize that men think differently than women do. That will sometimes make it difficult for you to understand his way of perceiving a situation; however, it's often just as difficult for him to understand *your* way of thinking.

That's another reason good communication is so important. As you and your husband communicate, you will begin to understand one another better. You will begin to understand why he thinks and reacts the way he does. In turn, he will begin to understand why you think and react the way *you* do. This is how you bring balance to one another in the realm of the soul.

Your husband will have the assurance that even if he makes a mistake you will not condemn him or put him down, because you are his friend. You understand him. All you want to do is talk to him and pray with him about the situation so he can come out on the other side in victory. And you know that he will do the same for you if you ever face a failure or disappointment. That is what true friends are for.

Here is another word of caution: Do not let your marriage relationship become "old hat" just because you begin to understand your husband better. If you are not careful, you can begin thinking, *I always know exactly what he's going to do. Tomorrow morning he'll get up and immediately take a shower. Then he'll shave and comb his hair. Then he'll put on his clothes and go downstairs to eat breakfast. I wish he was less predictable.*

It becomes easy to take your mate for granted when you start thinking that way. Do not let that happen. Your marriage is not just a routine thing. It's a gift from God, a union that should always bring both of you pleasure as you share in an endless process of giving and receiving.

As a godly wife, you should always remember that you need to be willing to give first because you were made for man. That does not mean your marriage is a one-way street where you have to do everything and your husband does nothing. It also does not mean you have to cater to your husband until you do not even feel like you are an individual anymore. What it *does* mean is this: You must seek the wisdom of God so you can walk forth in the ability He has given you and become the wife He has created you to be.

Your husband may be very different from you in personality, in temperament, and in the way he thinks. That does not matter when you are doing what you know to do in the spiritual, soul, and physical realms of your marriage relationship. Your obedience moves your marriage toward the goal of a complete union, where you and your husband can live in harmony, bound together by the love of God.

This is the way God created man and woman to be. So don't settle for anything less for *your* marriage.

Part III

ॐ

A Mother by Blessing

9

TRAIN UP YOUR CHILD IN THE LORD

We have talked about what it means to be the woman and the wife God created you to be. Now let's look at what the Bible says about the role of the Christian mother. Just as you are a woman by birth and a wife by choice, you are a mother by blessing.

Psalm 127:3 KJV says, "Lo, children are an heritage of the Lord: and the fruit of the womb is his reward." Genesis 33:5 KJV says, "And he lifted up his eyes, and saw the women and the children; and said, Who are those with thee? And he said, The children which God hath graciously given thy servant."

I want to show you something profound that God says about His role in your child's life:

> Thus says the Lord, your Redeemer, and He Who formed you from the womb: I am the Lord, Who made all things (Isa. 44:24).

Look at that phrase "He Who formed you from the womb." I want you to understand that the life in your womb is being formed by Almighty God Himself. That little spirit is alive unto God. Yes, you are your child's life-giving source in the natural. But in the spiritual realm, God is the One forming him or her.

That is why it is so important that you continually speak forth the Word of God to your child as he or she is being formed in the womb. Do not wait until you hold that child in your arms. Speak the Word over your child from the time you are aware of his or her conception. Speak what God says about your child, because God and His Word are one.

Speak forth the goodness of God. Speak forth that your child is alive unto God. Speak forth that your child is just like his or her Maker, that he or she is healthy, strong, and perfect because God is forming your child. As you continue to speak forth the truth about your child from the moment you know he or she is being formed in your womb, the truth will prevail in your child's life.

Don't make the mistake of being too caught up in natural issues, wondering, *Do I want my baby to be a boy or a girl? Do I want twins?* This basic truth of speaking the Word over your child is of much greater importance in light of eternity.

Your faithfulness to speak the Word will ensure that every door is closed to the enemy's attack. Then you will always have the assurance that your child is perfect and whole. You will not have to struggle with thoughts of worry when you hear negative things that people around you might say.

You have planted in your heart the knowledge that God is forming the life within you. You have faithfully spoken His Word over your child; therefore, you can rest in the confidence that when your baby is delivered, he or she will be perfect, whole, and complete.

From the time your child is born into this earth, his or her spirit is alive unto God. So keep on speaking the Word over your child from the time you hold him or her in your arms. Whisper in your child's ear that God is his or her Creator and Father and that Jesus is the Lord of your home.

Jesus showed compassion for the children.

At the same time came the disciples unto Jesus, saying, Who is the greatest in the kingdom of heaven? And Jesus called a little child unto him, and set him in the midst of them, and said, Verily I say unto you, Except ye be converted, and become as little children, ye shall not enter into the kingdom of heaven. Whosoever therefore shall humble himself as this little child, the same is greatest in the kingdom of heaven. And whoso shall receive one such little child in my name receiveth me. But whoso shall offend one of these little ones which believe in me, it were better for him that a millstone were hanged about his neck, and that he were drowned in the depth of the sea (Matt. 18:1-6 KJV).

You are to train up your child in the way he or she should go all the way from the womb into young adulthood. Proverbs 22:6 KJV says, "Train up a child in the way he should go...." Paul refers to the way Timothy was trained from childhood in the things of God:

> And how from your childhood you have had a knowledge of and been acquainted with the sacred Writings, which are able to instruct you and give you the understanding for salvation which comes through faith in Christ Jesus [through the leaning of the entire human personality on God in Christ Jesus in absolute trust and confidence in His power, wisdom, and goodness] (2 Tim. 3:15).

As a child, I was trained up in the Lord just as this verse describes. I cannot tell you the moment I received Christ because I was so young, but I know I did. I remember the awareness of it. Loving Jesus was always a way of life for me because I was taught the Gospel from the time I was very small.

All the memories I have of my childhood are within the context of a home that was full of love because God was there. As I was growing up, our home was also a place where the Word of God was continually being read, taught, and experienced.

That is the way it should be in your home. You need to provide a spiritual inheritance for your children.

When I came of age, I thought I knew everything, as most teenagers do, so I strayed from my spiritual roots a little bit. However, I never strayed to the point that I turned my back on the truth, because it was too real in my heart. I knew the Word of God held life and truth. I knew it would work in my life if I would obey it. Therefore, I could not stray very far from it.

Most people might think I was never much of a sinner. As Buddy used to say, "Pat has always been 'Miss Goody Two-Shoes.'" However, in my eyes, I *was* a sinner because I did not always live up to the standards I had set for myself. I let other people influence me rather than allowing God to influence me. In the end, I always had to return to God, renew my fellowship, and then go on with Him.

That is the way your children will be when they are brought up in the things of God from the time you hold them in your arms. As you talk to them about Jesus and speak the Word to them, spiritual things will become as natural to them as natural things are to other children.

When your children fall down and get scraped, they'll only know one thing to do: "If it hurts, it's time to pray." They will not even look at what hurts to see if it feels better after they pray. They will just go on about their day, believing that they are healed. That is the way it should be with your children as you train them up in the way they should go.

Discipline Your Children

Many times it is difficult for us as mothers to accept our responsibility of exercising authority over our children. We want to leave the discipline of the children for Dad to take care of when he gets home. The truth is, we have just as much of a part in disciplining our children as our husbands do.

A Scripture that helped me a lot regarding this issue is Proverbs 8:14:

I have counsel and sound knowledge, I have understanding, I have might and power.

Every day for a very long time, I had to confess this over myself as a mother to build confidence in me that I could consistently discipline my children according to the Word of God. Through confessing this Scripture, consistency came, as well as the understanding that I had to use the authority God had given me to carry out my responsibilities as a mother to my children.

Yes, you have a responsibility to teach your children the Word from the time they are small. Yes, you have the responsibility to teach them that they are created by God and born of God. But it is also important that you discipline them, because that is what teaches them to be disciplined people.

Personally, I do not believe the importance of this issue can be overstated. You need to cultivate self-discipline within your children so they grow up with an understanding and respect for authority.

It was often very difficult for me to stand in the authority that was mine as a mother and discipline my children. I had more of the gentle nature of my father, Kenneth E. Hagin. It just seemed easier to be sweet to my children and let them go along their merry way rather than to confront them with the consequences of their offenses.

If you love your children completely, you will discipline them. The Bible says so. (Prov. 13:24.) Therefore, I want to share some Scriptures to help you in case you, too, have difficulty exercising your God-given authority as a mother.

Discipline your son while there is hope, but do not [indulge your angry resentments by undue chastisements and] set yourself to his ruin (Prov. 19:18).

This tells you that there is a proper way to discipline your children. You do not do it in anger or because of any resentment you might be harboring inside of you. You discipline because you love your children. You see their error, and you want to teach them right from wrong so they can be loving and obedient children.

Another Scripture goes along with that.

Fathers, do not irritate and provoke your children to anger [do not exasperate them to resentment], but rear them [tenderly] in the training and discipline and the counsel and admonition of the Lord (Eph. 6:4).

We are to calm ourselves down and let the love that is within us flow forth to our children; then we can discipline them properly.

If you try to correct your children in anger, you run a high risk of disciplining them incorrectly. Perhaps you feel frustrated over some negative things that have happened to you. Right then your child does something wrong that triggers that frustration and you take out the frustration you are feeling on your child.

Your child may have committed a small offense that required a quiet word of correction. Your fit of anger could bring fear to your child's heart through the wrong kind of discipline. Continuing to make that mistake will cause resentment in your child, and it will be to your ruin.

The way a child turns out reflects on his or her parents and not on the child. You need to remember that. Be cautious to always walk in love when you discipline your children. Speak calmly but with firm authority as you correct them. If an offense requires a spanking, do it in love and with the Word of God so your children know exactly where you are coming from.

My father never disciplined my brother, Ken, or me in any way without sitting us down and asking us, "Do you understand why you are being punished?" He would make us tell him what we had done wrong and why we were being disciplined. If we did not answer correctly, he would explain our offense to us. However, we still received our punishment.

That is the way you need to speak to your children when you discipline them. Do not get so carried away in trying to explain every little detail of the situation that the spanking never occurs. When that happens, the children will learn they can manipulate the situation to their advantage. They will think, *If Mommy thinks I don't understand, she'll sit down and start talking about it, and I'll never get the punishment I'm supposed to get.*

Children are smart. They know how to manipulate and maneuver their parents—especially Mommy because she is usually the one who is with them the most. That is why parents need to confess that they have knowledge, wisdom, and understanding in this area of disciplining their children.

As for my brother and me, we understood that our parents were the authority in the home, and we respected them. We knew their love for us was the reason they disciplined us. We understood that it was for our benefit because they were a lot older than we were. We were just children. They knew a lot more about life than we did. They could give us knowledge, understanding, and wisdom in every area of our lives. We also knew that we were in trouble if we did not obey their instruction.

Discipline With Purpose

Proverbs 10:12-13 says:

Hatred stirs up contentions, but love covers all transgressions. On the lips of him who has discernment skillful and godly Wisdom is found, but discipline and the rod are for the back of him who is without sense and understanding.

If you are disciplining your children in anger and bring them to the point of resentment, hatred eventually arises. In that hatred, there is contention, but the Bible says that love covers all transgressions.

Verse 13 goes on to say, "The rod is for the back of him who is without sense and understanding." Your children are not yet at a level of maturity where they have knowledge and understanding in many areas. That is why it is important that you impart knowledge unto them—often through discipline.

For some reason, and the reason is usually that they are like their mother or father, children are a little stubborn and quite determined to have their own way. That means you often have to penetrate that stubbornness with the rod on the backside. That is why Solomon wrote this proverb as a guideline for parents.

Please note, however, that this Scripture says the rod is for the *backside* of the person who lacks understanding and thus does wrong. There is a proper place on your child's body for the rod to be used, and that does *not* mean "whatever place is available." That is not proper discipline, and it is not disciplining in love.

When I was a child, I remember visiting a particular female relative whose form of disciplining her kids always unnerved and disturbed me. She would yell and scream and hit whatever part of the child's body that was nearest her.

I never could understand that kind of discipline. It always upset me and made me cry, although I was not involved in the situation. I was not used to that. I was disciplined in love, so my relative's yelling and screaming frightened me. It did not look like love to me.

When my dad spanked my brother or me, he would always tell us calmly to lay over the bed. Then he would give us a few licks with the rod. I just hated those spankings, and I did not get very many of them either. I learned quickly. My brother, on the other hand, took a long time to learn how to avoid them. Even when I was being spanked, though, I was aware that my parents were disciplining me in love.

So make sure you stay in love as you discipline your child. Remain calm, and let the love of God flow through you. Bring out the Word, and show them what God says about the importance of obedience to parents and the need for discipline.

I can remember what my mother would always say right before she spanked me: "I'm doing this because I love you." I would think, *Oh, sure you are!* But because my parents always gave me the Word before they disciplined me, there came a point in time when I understood my mother's words.

It is important to always calmly show your child the scriptural reason for the discipline you are about to administer. Even though this may be difficult for a young child to fully understand at first, just stay diligent in taking that extra time to explain from the Word.

As you do this, the time will come when your children will not only understand what you have been telling them, but they will appreciate it. And their respect for you will grow strong as they come to better understand your position of authority in their lives.

> He who spares his rod [of discipline] hates his son, but he who loves him disciplines diligently and punishes him early (Prov. 13:24).

The phrase "disciplines diligently and punishes him early" implies an earnestness on the part of parents[1] because they understand children need to learn self-discipline before foolish behaviors become bad habits.[2] Therefore, "discipline diligently" *doesn't* mean, "Johnny, if you do that again, I'm going to spank you. Johnny, I said if you do not stop that, I am going to spank you. Johnny, I'm going to count to three, and if you haven't stopped that, I'm going to spank you."

If you keep saying that all day long without ever following through on your words, Johnny will know that he can keep doing it as long as he wants to because you do not mean what you say. You are not being consistent in the discipline of your child.

Then after Johnny has continued to do what you told him not to, the time comes when you finally reach the point of irritation. You jerk him up, swing him around, and discipline him in a fit of anger. All you have done in this case is instill fear and resentment in Johnny because you are not being diligent and consistent in your discipline of him.

As my children were growing up, they knew they would be punished when they did something wrong. They also knew that Mama would wait until she could calmly discipline them.

I remember one Sunday morning when one of my daughters was not obedient. I was feeling uptight about the situation, but we were preparing for church and were not ones to be late. It was almost time to leave, so I looked at my daughter and said, "I will deal with you later when I'm calm and you've thought about it awhile."

So we went on our way to church and afterwards went out to lunch. On our way home, my daughter said, "Mommy, I've thought about it. Are you calm?" She wanted to get it over with. She knew I would never forget it.

Often a child will think, *Well, if I don't say anything about it, my mom will forget it.* But my children knew I didn't forget when they did something wrong. My dad had taught me, "Don't forget it; deal with it in love."

While I took the time to become calm before I disciplined my children, they had the time to think about what they did. They knew they were wrong. They knew that if I loved them, I would do exactly what I had said I would do. So when it came time to discipline them for that offense, it penetrated and taught them another lesson in obedience and respect.

The Bible says we are to discipline our children early. I received a lot of flack in raising my children because everyone thought my husband and I were too strict with our children in requiring obedience regarding what we told them to do. Buddy and I knew our children needed the principles of God to be formed in them, so we stayed consistent in what we expected of them.

Babies have tempers. Even when my children were small babies, they knew by the tone of my voice that when I said "Hush," I meant it, and even at that tender age they hushed. I found that it is all in the way a mother represents her authority to her children.

By the time my children were five or six months old, they were pulling themselves up into a standing position and beginning to walk. At this age, they understood what "no" meant. They understood what a little slap on the leg or the hand meant.

I was not abusing them. They were not left with any red mark. But they understood that Mama's slap meant "no."

I can remember the time we visited my cousin's house and my middle child, Cookie, was about seven months old. She kept crawling over to the record racks next to the stereo, where she would try to pull out the records from the rack.

The first time Cookie did this, I looked at her and said, "No." She moved her hand back and grinned at me. Then in a minute when she did not think I was looking, back that little hand went to try to pull out a record.

The second time she did this, I gave her a little slap on the hand and again said, "No." She moved her hand back and crawled away. Then she looked up at me and grinned, as if to say, "Oh, I'm so sweet, Mommy."

You know how babies do. They are so cute, it is difficult to do anything but smile at them. But they will not be cute for long if you do not discipline them.

It took Cookie awhile to learn her lesson that day. She tried another five or six times to pull out those records. Every time I would give her a little slap on the hand and say, "I said no."

Many parents would have said, "Oh, she's just a baby." Then they would pick up all the records and put them where their child could not reach them.

That is not teaching your child properly. If you're always putting "no-no's" out of reach, there will come a day when you go to someone's house that *hasn't* been "child-proofed." Then your child will embarrass you because he or she won't understand the meaning of the word "no."

This is why many parents never take their children anywhere with them. Every time they do, their children embarrass them. That is a disgrace to the parents.

People are aware of your family. They are aware of whether or not your children behave. They know why you never have your children with you, especially if they have ever been in your home. I know that sounds hard, but it is true.

After a while, Cookie finally got the message, as I stayed consistent. She crawled off and found her toys that she was supposed to be playing with and played happily with them.

You have to be that diligent and consistent in disciplining your children as well. You instill within them the principles of obedience and respect for authority that are so crucial for success in life.

Another important passage of Scripture is in Proverbs 23:12-14. My dad used to share this Scripture with my brother and me before he disciplined us.

Apply your mind to instruction and correction and your ears to words of knowledge. Withhold not discipline from the child; for if you strike and punish him with the [reedlike] rod, he will not die. You shall whip him with the rod and deliver his life from Sheol (Hades, the place of the dead).

Notice what the first part of verse 12 says: "Apply your mind to instruction and correction." That is the message you need to tell your children repeatedly as they grow toward adulthood.

You can also see once again how important it is that you spare not the rod in your home. However, make sure you administer that necessary discipline God's way and not your own carnal way.

God chastises us by His Word, and He always does it lovingly. Although the Word is gentle, simple, and kind, it sure can hurt as it penetrates our hearts with conviction. When that happens, we know we have been chastised.

That is the way we should be with our children. Their sore backsides make them aware that they have been chastised. They understand that it was for their own good, and eventually they will choose to do something about it because the spanking was administered gently and calmly in love.

Don't Break Your Child's Spirit

Just as God gently chastises us with His Word, you should always deal gently with your children, not only in your mannerisms but also with your tongue. As Proverbs 15:4 says, "A gentle tongue [with its healing power] is a tree of life, but willful contrariness in it breaks down the spirit."

Sometimes you may say something in correction to your child that is not wrong, but the tone of your voice is inappropriate and displeasing to God. When that happens, your words fail to correct and teach your child; instead, they help break down your child's spirit.

When the Bible speaks of discipline, it never speaks of breaking a child's spirit or will. It speaks of molding the child's spirit according to the Word.

That child's free will is all God has to work with because the child will exercise his or her will to choose between life or death—between the way of the Word or the way of the world. Therefore, if someone breaks a child's will, that child will not be able to understand how to make that decision for him- or herself.

Many times children whose spirits have been broken spend the rest of their lives in mental institutions or in special homes for the emotionally disturbed. Professionals try to rebuild these broken people because of what someone took out of them when they were young. That restoration will never take place if the truth of God's Word is not used to restore these people to wholeness. They will never be able to respond to God in a way that brings deliverance and healing.

Be cautious to discipline your child in love and with a gentle tongue of instruction. Then your child will come out of that time of correction knowing what he or she should do and how to do it—strengthened in spirit and in will to do right.

Teach Your Children To Behave in Public

Parents also have to teach their children how to dress and behave in public. The common failure of parents to teach this to their children used to really irritate me as I was growing up. My brother and I did not always have many clothes, but what we had was always clean and put together properly. My mother never let us go out of the house if we did not look nice.

When we went to other ministers' homes, it always amazed me to see how often the children looked like orphans. Their clothes were dirty and torn. They may have had one shoe on with a sock and the other shoe on with no sock. Their hair did not look like it had been combed all day. These children had not been taught how to dress.

Ken and I were taught to take pride in how we looked. I would wear a little skirt and matching blouse; he would wear a nice pair of pants and a matching shirt. We were always neat and clean, and our hair was always combed.

Sometimes we would go to lunch with these ministers, and I remember my mother asking the other parents, "Would you like me to help you get your children ready to go?"

"Oh, we're not going to take them," they would reply. "There is bologna in the refrigerator. They can fix themselves a sandwich when they get hungry. They don't act like your children in public."

I used to think, *What poor children.* It was a treat for me to go out to eat with my parents, because at that time we did not get to do it very often.

My parents took pride in me, knowing that I knew how to behave myself. I knew when to talk and when to be quiet. When they said to sit still, I knew how to sit still.

I knew my parents meant what they said. So no matter what I was doing at that moment, if they told me to stop, I stopped and sat still. I was not afraid of them; I just understood that they were the authority and that I was to respect that fact.

Repeatedly, I observed parents who neglected their children, leaving them at home because they had not been taught how to behave. Many of these children grew up to be rebellious adults because they believed their parents loved the people they ministered to more than they loved their own children.

These ministers' children grew up full of resentment toward Christians and devoid of all respect for their parents. Many of them ended up as alcoholics. Others were killed in car accidents while in a drunken state before they turned twenty years old.

I heard those parents ask my folks, "What did we do wrong? Look at your children. They are serving God. They understand authority. They have respect for themselves and for others. Why did my child turn out differently?"

When parents have just lost a child and then start asking you these kinds of questions, you cannot begin to tell them all they have done wrong. That is the wrong time to do it. You have to speak in love, sharing with them what you have done right as a parent rather than what they have done wrong. Often they get the message, but by then it is too late for the child they have lost.

That is why the Bible says to be diligent to discipline your children while they are young. Do not wait until your child is thirteen and fourteen years old before you decide to make him or her obey you. Then it will be too late.

Parents Must Be Established in the Word

I want to point out a few other common parenting pitfalls that we should make every effort to avoid. First, our children suffer if we as parents are not diligent to establish ourselves in the Word. If we are not established, we will not know how to establish them in the Word. Therefore, fear reigns supreme in our lives and in our homes. On the inside of us, we know we are not doing the right thing. We know we have not been the examples we should be, for our motto has been "Do as I say and not as I do."

Living that kind of example before your children will not give them the discipline they need to prepare for life. Yes, your children need your love and understanding, but only as it is based on the Word of God. The only way to answer that need is to first make sure you yourself are established in the Word; then you must discipline your children according to what you know God has said.

Many times I have seen the frustration of children who constantly try to please their parents but can never live up to their expectations. No matter what they do, it is always wrong.

These parents criticize and seldom praise their children. The children long for one gentle word of encouragement but never hear it. Therefore, these children become cowed down. After a while, their wills become broken.

At that point, the hard-to-please parents have a mess on their hands that they do not know how to fix. They may realize the problem lies with them but are unsure of what they can do about it.

Many times children who have parents like this are scarred for life. Unless these children get into the Word of God as they should and let the Spirit of God work in them, they may never overcome some of the scars and hurts inflicted by bad parenting. Don't be hard to please.

Mother and Father Should Agree in Discipline

As a mother, you may be with your children more than your husband because he is out making a living to provide for his family. Therefore, it may seem as if the responsibility for your children's discipline rests with you more than with him.

If you and your husband maintain good communication, then that is not true. You should discuss the subject of disciplining the children at length. You should know what he thinks about it, and you should agree.

You and your husband need to be in unity about disciplining the children so you do not have to say, "Just wait until your daddy gets home." When you say that to your children, you are making Daddy look like the bad guy. Daddy is not the bad guy, and neither are you. However, that tactic makes it appear that way to your children.

You have as much responsibility as the father does in disciplining, teaching, and instructing your children. Discuss this subject with your husband, agree on how to discipline the children, and then enforce what you have agreed upon, instead of waiting until their daddy comes home.

Never correct your husband regarding the way he disciplines the children while you are in their presence. Whether he's right or wrong, don't do it, because the children will learn that they can manipulate Mom against Dad to get what they want because Mom is not in agreement.

I have seen this situation many times. The father disciplines the child, but as soon as Daddy is gone, Mama has the child in her lap, loving on him and saying, "Well, that mean old daddy. Here's a lollipop, honey. It'll be all right."

If you are doing that, you're undermining your husband's authority in your child's eyes. You are not teaching your child the way of the Word. Instead, you are leading your child down a path of rebellion that leads to destruction.

If you do not agree with the way your husband has disciplined the children in a particular situation, discuss it with him later in private. Talk to him about it quietly and calmly until you can come to an agreeable conclusion. That way you can maintain a unified front before your children.

Ask Your Child To Forgive You

If you are the one who has disciplined your child incorrectly, do not be ashamed to go to that child and ask for forgiveness. Rest assured that your child is already aware of what you did wrong. Therefore, you might as well be big enough to say, "I'm sorry. I did not discipline you correctly. Please forgive me."

When you do that, you form a strong bond between you and your child that will never be broken. Your child understands, *Yes, Mom does love me. She does have a desire to discipline me by the Word; otherwise, she wouldn't have asked me to forgive her.* A child responds to that kind of openness in his or her parents.

You are to live a godly example before your children. When you do something wrong in discipline and then ask them to forgive you, you are teaching them humility.

I have often asked my children to forgive me. It was not difficult, because my heart was right before God. I also wanted everything to be right in my household. Do not let those mess-ups slip by and think, *Oh, well, they're just children. They don't know.*

Yes, they do know. Children are very sensitive. They know when they are being treated right and when they are not. It is up to us as parents to check ourselves and make sure we are walking in love and disciplining our children according to the Word.

As you train up your children in the ways of the Lord, you should keep Ephesians 6:1-3 in the center of everything you say to them.

My dad used to ask Ken and me all the time, "Do you know what the first commandment with promise is?"

Oh, yes, we knew. The minute Dad began to say that, we knew what was coming. He wanted us to start quoting Ephesians 6:1-3:

Children, obey your parents in the Lord [as His representatives], for this is just and right. Honor (esteem and value as precious) your father and your mother—this is the first commandment with a promise—that all may be well with you and that you may live long on the earth.

Imprint this passage of Scripture on your children's spirits. I guarantee you, Ken and I knew it by heart. When our dad asked us if we knew what that first commandment with promise said, we always responded, "Yes, we know."

Dad would always reply, "All right. Then tell me what it says."

That was hard for us as children to want to quote that Scripture passage repeatedly. By requiring us to do that, our dad was gradually building within us understanding, respect, and godly character.

Do the same thing with your children. Do not have the attitude that says, "Well, I don't have time to teach my children the Word like that." You had better take the time, unless you want you and your children to experience unnecessary heartache and disappointment.

Often young people who come from Christian families get into trouble with drugs, alcohol, and unwanted pregnancies because they were not disciplined properly. They were never molded with the Word of God. They did not have godly character built into them, because their parents did not take the time to do it. Their parents were too busy with their own lives.

That is not the way of the Word. If you are going to follow God's plan for you as a mother, you will have to walk in the scriptural knowledge you have about parenting. At the same time, you should always strive to excel even more. This is how you begin to attain God's highest in the quest to train up your children in the way they should go.

Train Up Your Child in Keeping With His Gift

Notice what the following verse says.

Train up a child in the way he should go [and in keeping with his individual gift or bent], and when he is old he will not depart from it (Prov. 22:6).

Part of training your child in the way he should go is to train him in keeping with his individual gift or bent.

I will use my son, Damon, as an example. Damon is very creative. His mind is going all the time. He is always thinking of things to do. When he was young, that creativity had to be channeled. We had to teach him discipline in keeping with his individual gift. We did not destroy his creativity, but we channeled it through discipline, love, understanding, and knowledge.

That is what you have to do with your child. Each child has a gift—an individual gift within that will cause him or her to excel in life, if it is channeled properly with godly discipline according to the Word of God.

So this verse is saying, "Teach your child in the way he or she should go according to his or her individual gifts. If you will do that, then when your child is old, he or she will not depart from what you have taught him or her."

As you point your child in the right direction, he or she will continue to go forward in that divinely appointed direction where his or her individual gifts are excelling rather than being ignored or destroyed within.

Do as I Do

The Word of God contains all the knowledge you need to discipline your children and successfully train them up in the ways of the Lord. I am not telling you anything new in this book, but I want to stir you up so you will evaluate yourself.

- Are you really doing everything you know to do as a mother?

- Are you being consistent?

- Are you walking in your role as a mother in the fullness God intended for you?

- Are you molding your children's character to reflect the character of God?

- Are you being a godly example to your children? Or are you telling them, "Don't do as I do; do as I say"?

No matter what you say, your children are going to follow what you do. As you line up what you do with the Word you speak, your children will learn the ways of the Lord even as they imitate your actions.

Be diligent to discipline your children while they are young. Do not neglect an all-important responsibility God has given you.

We have all seen the results in this country of a generation of parents who neglected their God-given responsibility to discipline their children. These parents were products of the permissive parenting philosophy that said, "Your children have minds of their own. So instead of spanking them, let them do their own thing."

The children grew up and did their own thing, all right. On college campuses all over the nation, they wreaked havoc and destruction during the late '60s and early '70s because their parents had not disciplined them when they were wrong.

These young people had no respect for anyone or anything. They did not understand authority. In the end, the rebellion of that generation helped to further the erosion of such basic values as honor and integrity, which have kept our country strong since its birth more than two and a quarter centuries ago.

Parenting is serious business, my friend. It is *God's* business. It is good to know God has given you everything you need to be the godly mother He has created you to be. You have all the abilities, all the knowledge, and all the authority you could ever need to train up your children properly in the Lord. Put all that spiritual parenting equipment to practice, and watch it work in your home.

10

PRACTICAL PARENTING BY GOD'S WORD

We chose to create our children. In making that choice, we assumed the responsibility that goes along with it. How our children turn out is on our shoulders as parents.

Proverbs 20:11 says, "Even a child is known by his acts, whether [or not] what he does is pure and right." Many times we see a child act up in public and think, *Well, I know how that child is disciplined at home.* We say that because the child's behavior reveals the child's home life.

It is crucial to teach your children how to respect authority and behave properly, whether at home or in public. Along this line, I want to give you some more practical guidelines that will help you achieve your goal of raising obedient, respectful children into godly, successful adults.

I recommend you explain to your children how spiritual principles always have a natural parallel. For instance, you want them to be good stewards of the gifts and talents God has given them in life. Therefore, prepare them to be good stewards by helping them understand how to take care of their possessions.

Teach your children that the things they have were given to them to be cared for. Show them that they must be good stewards in every area of their lives, with everything they have, and in everything they do.

I was sharing this with a lady one time, and she said, "Are you serious about what you're saying?"

I said, "Of course I am. I have given you Scriptures. It's the Word of God."

"Well, no wonder I don't have anything," she exclaimed.

"What do you mean?" I asked.

She replied, "My husband has worked hard, and we have a nice home, but our furniture and our carpet are in shambles. I just let my kids go all through the house with food. They jump on the couch and on the bed. They play everywhere. I was raised that way, and I never thought about it before. Isn't that terrible to be my age and yet still have a home that is always in shambles because I've been in ignorance?"

Some people do not understand the value of stewardship. They think that being careless with one's possessions is the only way to live because they were brought up that way. They do not learn by being around other people who live differently. They just think, *Well, I am the way I am because of the way I was raised and because of what I was taught.*

The devil would like them to think that. In a chaotic home environment, the enemy has greater opportunity to bring division and strife in order to tear that family apart.

Teach your children to take care of their bodies. Teach them also to take care of their toys, their clothes, and their furniture.

Many people thought Buddy and I were so strict as parents for this reason. If my children wanted to eat a snack or have something to drink, they sat at the kitchen table. That was the purpose of the table, not the purpose of my furniture.

People thought it was cruel of me to make my children eat at the kitchen table. I would say to those people, "What's cruel about it? That is how my parents taught me, and I was not ever hindered by that restriction. I never became rebellious or resentful because I could not go to the living room couch and eat my cookie. I knew that if I was going to eat, I stayed in the kitchen and sat at the table. That was what the table was for. Then if I left crumbs or my drink spilled, the mess was on the table and was easy to clean up. To me, that is using common sense."

Teach your children that the couch is to sit on and not to stand on. Teach them that the bed is to lie on and not to jump on. If they want to jump, they can go outside. If they want to ride something like a horse, buy them a "horse-stick" or a rocking horse so they can focus their energy in the proper place.

You are teaching them to have respect for and to take care of the things they have.

You have worked hard for the material possessions you own. Obtaining these things did not come easily, and your children need to understand that.

Many young people believe that the world owes them a living and that anything they want should just be handed to them. Do not let your children grow up with that attitude. It is your job to teach them responsibility. You should instill within them the knowledge that they have the ability to be thoughtful, respectful people who understand the importance of faithful stewardship.

Keep a Right Confession

We have talked about how important it is for you to speak the Word over your children from the womb on into adulthood. That is a vital part of training them up in the way they should go. Even if your child seems to be taking a wrong direction in life, *you must keep your confession right.*

Many parents say, "I taught my children about the Lord when they were very young, but look at them now. They're not living for the Lord." What they do not understand is that their wrong confession can hinder their children from coming back to the Lord.

My husband lived the first few years of his life with his grandfather, a Pentecostal minister. Buddy's grandfather would always conduct daily devotions for his little grandson, during which they would share the Word and pray together. When a challenging situation arose, his grandfather would always quote the Word. As a result, Buddy got full of the Word as a child.

Later Buddy went back to live in his father's home, where the atmosphere was remarkably different. His father had stopped living for the Lord and had gone the way of the world. Buddy tried to go that way too, but the Word in him was too great. He was continually drawn back to the truth. He could never find happiness in his father's footsteps, because the Word was imbedded in his spirit.

That is why I am stressing to you to continually share the Word with your children. Then say, "Father, I have done as Your Word tells me to do. I have trained up my children in the way they should go. They know the Word because it's been planted in their spirits."

If it seems that your children are straying from the Word in their later years, you can add, "Even though the Word is lying dormant in their spirits right now, I know it is there. I know in the name of Jesus that their spirits will awaken and follow after the truth."

The Word works. No matter how bad the circumstances may seem, your child will follow what he has been taught. Do not set your eyes on the circumstances. Instead, make this your confession: "Lord, I did as the Word says. Therefore, what You have promised regarding my children is already done." You will maintain a calmness and strength within you that helps you stand fast in faith for the restoration of your children.

Don't Expect Perfection

As you endeavor to discipline and train your children properly, do not be overly self-conscious about their behavior if it is not always perfect.

I had this problem concerning my children. Maybe it stemmed from my past. People always seemed to expect me to be prim and proper because I was the minister's daughter.

When you have a self-conscious attitude about your children, you have a tendency to withdraw and hold them to yourself, not letting anyone else see how they can act sometimes.

Personally, I almost reached the point of getting physically sick over this issue. I finally had to say, "Lord, forgive me. I am wrong."

God showed me that children are children, and no matter how well we teach them, they are still going to do and say things we do not want them to do or say.

Here is a wonderful Scripture to confess about your children, even when their outward behavior does not seem to line up with its truth:

> The father of the [uncompromisingly] righteous (the upright, in right standing with God) shall greatly rejoice, and he who becomes the father of a wise child shall have joy in him. Let your father and your mother be glad, and let her who bore you rejoice (Prov. 23:24,25).

When children experience the benefits of doing what the Word says, they often develop their own desire to do the right thing. Fear of punishment is not their motivation anymore.

They obey because they know their parents love them and they love their parents as well.

Most of the things young children do wrong are unintentional. After all, they are just children and they have much to learn.

That is why we need to have the Word continually flowing in our homes even while our children are still in the womb. Good teaching begins at home and reaches into every area of their lives. Ultimately, as you discipline your children and share the Scriptures with them in love, you will see results.

As time goes on and your children reach school age, they will begin to understand that you discipline them because you love them. You will become not only their mother but also their friend.

My girls would come home and tell me everything that was said or done at school, from elementary school on. That's why I know what I'm talking about when I say that sometimes it's difficult not to react to what your children say to you. Do your best to stay calm and understanding, because the wrong kind of reaction will only serve to shut down your line of communication with them.

You can say things like, "I don't think that's something a child of God should be saying. I respect and love you, and I don't want you saying that because I want other people to respect you as well."

What you do not have to say is, "I don't want to hear that word come out of your mouth again. That's a dirty word."

Kids hear dirty words at school every day. Once a child's curiosity is aroused, that child will want to hear every dirty word there is. That is how most kids are.

You have to learn to use wisdom and stay calm. You can even act casual and say, "Yes, I've heard that before. So what?" Meanwhile, on the inside you are thinking, *I cannot believe that just came out of my child's mouth.*

Today children learn young. Some of the things my girls heard in elementary school, I did not hear until I was in junior high.

I once had a teacher tell me that if you make it through your children's junior high years without too many disasters, you have got it made. At the time, I thought, *What is she talking about?* I soon learned! I praise God for the wisdom of the Word, because it sure delivered me out of many tight places as a mother.

Respond to Your Children's Questions

You do not have to be ashamed to say to your adolescent child, "I'm not sure of the answer now, so I am going to pray to make sure I give you the right answer." However, you shouldn't say, "Well, I don't know, so don't worry about it." That is no answer at all—especially to a teenager.

After you tell your child, "Don't do this," and they ask, "Why?" do not allow yourself to say, "Because I said so." Whether or not your children will like what you have to say, give them a real answer. If they do not get answers from you, they will go elsewhere to get them.

I have counseled teenagers whose parents told them, "You're not old enough to understand." If children are old enough to ask, they are old enough to understand.

When your children come to you for answers, get your Bible out and look for what God says about their questions. Then express the answer in the simplest way you can. Teach them to look to the Word and to you for their answers so they do not ask someone else. They should trust you for the truth.

Teach Personal Hygiene to Your Children

So many children feel condemned when they become teenagers because they start having thoughts about their own bodies or the bodies of others. If you have taught your children properly, they will know where those thoughts are coming from and what to do about them. And if they ever have a problem in this area, they will come to you for help.

Never allow your child to be ashamed of his or her body. God made the physical body. He put every part together, and every part has a specific purpose. Present it this way to your child, and your child will grow up understanding in a healthy way what the body is for.

One aspect of teaching your children about their bodies is training them in personal hygiene. For instance, so many girls do not know anything about the menstrual cycle because their mothers have never talked to them about it. The thought scares these adolescent girls because they do not understand that it is a normal part of growing up.

Now, it's true that most schools show films in gym classes that explain the process of going through puberty. However, it is much better for girls to learn about this subject from their mothers.

Some mothers think, *My daughter probably won't begin menstruating until she is twelve, so I'll wait until then to talk to her about it.* Don't wait! It is surprising how young some girls are when they begin their monthly cycles. If your daughter happens to be one of those girls, you don't want her to have that experience without the knowledge she needs to help her get through it.

When I became pregnant with our son, Damon, my daughters were eight and ten. They were very curious and wanted to know why a baby was growing on the inside of me.

If your children want to know, you have to tell them. Take out your Bible and begin in Genesis 1. Explain that God made Adam; then He saw that Adam needed a woman to make him happy. You can go from there to explain the whole process that leads to the birth of a new life.

It is best if your children can hear these things from you. Before I was pregnant with Damon, a friend of my older daughter, Candy, told her about her teenage sister. Her sister's boyfriend came over to their house while their mother was at work. Candy's friend went on to tell all that her older sister and her boyfriend did together at the house.

From the younger sister's perspective, what she was observing was unpleasant. The situation was helped immensely when I shared on the same subject from a scriptural perspective with my daughters.

When you share with your children on this subject, use medical terms instead of slang words. If you do not know the right terms, get a medical book and learn them.

I tried to be very open with my girls in every area, including our discussions about sex. Earlier generations were very inhibited about this subject. But in the age we are living in, it seems the Holy Spirit is bringing forth greater understanding in every area of life—spirit, soul, and body.

Make Your Home a Happy Home

I know it is not always easy to keep your home in order. We live in a world where so often both the husband and the wife work and the kids are involved in all sorts of extracurricular activities.

Often the result of all this busyness is that the home becomes a house. No one ever eats together. All the family members come in late from their activities, retreat to their rooms, and go to bed. Then they get up the next morning and start all over again. That isn't a home; it's a house being used as a way station.

As a mother, you should do everything within your power to maintain a happy home life, in which family members regularly enjoy times of fellowship and fun together. That is what I did as Buddy and I raised our children in the admonition of the Lord.

My children were involved in after-school activities. However, I never allowed them to get involved in so many things that we could not have a home life.

The tendency today is for parents to think that the more activities their children can be involved in, the better it will be for them in life. The number of extracurricular activities becomes the measuring stick of how talented the children are compared to other children. That is a lie of the enemy.

A strong family is more important than any football game, cheerleading practice, or dance lesson. Make sure your family regularly spends time together. Ask God to help you and your husband establish a balance that allows your family to spend quality time together. Remember that you are both responsible before God for your children's spiritual and emotional welfare, and that includes maintaining a strong home life.

If possible, dinnertime should be reserved as family time. The meal may be a simple crock pot creation, but take the time to sit down with your family and eat that meal.

It blesses me when my children say that some of their best memories of home are the times we sat around the dinner table having a good time as a family, laughing and talking about the things that happened during the day. These precious times of enjoying each other's company strengthened our family unit.

Stand in the Gap for Your Children

We have talked about many practical guidelines that will help you be the mother God created you to be. There is nothing more beneficial or powerful you can do for your children than to intercede for them every day.

You should begin every day by praying, "Father, I thank You this day that my home is perfected. I thank You that my children will walk in peace and joy and love today."

Then begin to intercede for them. If they are in school, you should take authority in the name of Jesus over the evil forces that would try to come against them. Stand your ground knowing that they are protected because you have called forth that divine protection in faith. Make this a way of life.

Do not put off praying for your child until you sense urgency in your spirit. Don't wait until Susie is really acting strange and you are wondering, *Why is she acting that way?* How long has it been since you prayed for her?

Prayer keeps your home full of joy, peace, love, and understanding. As you pray daily for your family, your spirit lives big in you. You act according to the Word rather than according to your feelings. You respond according to your spirit rather than your carnal mind or the world's standards because your spirit dominates you. This gives you confidence to know you are walking according to what God has said.

During my early years of marriage, when Buddy was out of fellowship with the Lord, many situations arose in which I did not know what to do. I looked to the Holy Spirit, my Comforter, and interceded for Buddy and our home.

If you find yourself feeling the same way, start praying in the Spirit and confessing the wisdom of God. Speak forth by faith:

"I'm a child of God, and I have the Holy Spirit. I know when I pray in the Spirit, I'm praying the perfect prayer. Therefore, the Holy Spirit is at work in my home. I confess His wisdom; therefore, I will know what to do and when to do it; I will know what to say and what not to say. I will work alongside my husband, and we will be united in every area of our lives together."

Confess God's divine promises. They are part of your spiritual inheritance in Christ. If you confess them, they will work in your home, and your household can be spared from continual strife and upheaval.

Rely on the Holy Spirit's direction. Sometimes during the day, a thought may come to you about your child. Most people think, *Oh, that's just me; I'm such a protective mother.* Many times it is the Holy Spirit prompting you to intercede. Perhaps your child is having a problem in school, and God wants you to intervene on his or her behalf.

In some schools, evil spirits are actually assigned to come against children who know the Lord. Many times when my children came home from school, I would know as soon as they walked through the door that a spirit had been harassing them that day.

When that happens, you have to take authority over these evil spirits and say, "You don't belong in my home, and you have no right to harass my child. This home belongs to the Father God, and in the name of Jesus you cannot stay here!"

Use your authority every day that Jesus gave you in His name. That is a simple way to say it, but it is the truth.

So many times we think our child's wrong behavior is "only a phase." It is true that every child goes through certain phases, but you do not have to put up with one disaster after another.

When it is evident that the enemy is harassing your child, help him or her understand what is going on and then deal with the situation. Sit down with your child and read the Scripture that pertains to the situation; then take authority over the problem in Jesus' name. This can actually be a time in which you and your child grow closer through the experience.

If your child is of elementary school age or even younger, you can take authority over evil spirits without his or her knowledge and eliminate any possibility of fear. Then you can take your child lovingly in your arms and say, "In the name of Jesus, Father, I thank You that my child is surrounded with peace, love, and joy."

Walk in Your Authority

Walk in your authority on a daily basis as the mother of your children. As they are leaving for school, take authority over any evil force that would try to come against them that day. Then stand your ground, knowing that the blood of Jesus protects them because they are in your household and you are of the household of God.

In Exodus 12:1-30, we read that the blood of the Passover lamb applied to the door posts of the Israelites' homes protected all those who were in the homes the night the death angel passed over Egypt. John 1:29 tells us Jesus is the Lamb of God.

Hebrews chapters 9 and 10 tell us His blood is better than the blood of bulls, goats, or the Passover lamb.

If the blood of animals in the Old Testament provided such great protection and cleansing, how much more does the blood of Jesus do for us? When you pray for your children and apply the blood of Jesus over them, you can stand in confidence knowing they walk in the protection of God.

Your measuring line for success in your home should not be what you or the world thinks—but what God thinks according to His Word. Discover His perspective; then you can create your world from that divine perspective by faithfully confessing God's promises for your home and family.

As you walk in obedience to what God has said about you as a woman, a wife, and a mother, you will realize your dream of a happy, godly home. Your children *will* be a part of the kingdom of God, if for no other reason than the truth that the Word of God says so and you believe the Word.

11

THE VIRTUOUS WOMAN REVEALED

Proverbs 31 gives us a vivid picture of the virtuous woman. This word picture is in many ways a summary of the scriptural principles of womanhood that we've discussed. As women, we need to carefully study this passage of Scripture so we can learn how to live as virtuous women, wives, and mothers according to God's definition.

The writer starts with a wonderful tribute to the worth of a woman who fits the description given in verses 10-12:

A capable, intelligent, and virtuous woman—who is he who can find her? She is far more precious than jewels and her value is far above rubies or pearls.

The heart of her husband trusts in her confidently and relies on and believes in her securely, so that he has no lack of [honest] gain or need of [dishonest] spoil.

She comforts, encourages, and does him only good as long as there is life within her.

Verse 12 describes your God-ordained job as a wife in a nutshell—assisting, aiding, encouraging, and comforting your husband.

She Cares About Her Family's Appearance

Now let's look at verse 13: "She seeks out wool and flax and works with willing hands [to develop it]." The virtuous woman is careful to ensure that her family looks nice and has the material things they need.

Many times people adopt an "I don't care" attitude because they are not as prosperous as those around them are. They say, "Everyone knows I don't have much, so why should I try to look neat and clean?"

It does not matter what your financial status is, your children can still look neat and clean. You can give them the best you can for your economic level. You can take care of their clothes by laundering them properly and ironing them. You can take care of their shoes and accessories. And as they grow older, you can teach them to do the same.

If your husband does not know how to coordinate his different articles of clothing, help him. If he puts on a wrong combination, just tell him sweetly, "Honey, I don't think that tie goes with that suit. Another one might look better." You do not have to say, "That tie looks horrible."

The same rule applies to your children. Show an interest in them. Tell them they should want to look nice because they are children of the King.

Some parents think, *Oh well. He is just a kid. Who cares what he looks like?* Your child may be "just a kid," but he has feelings too.

You should take pride in keeping your home clean and orderly. This establishes you as an effective witness.

Your home shouldn't have toys scattered all over the living room floor, cracker crumbs littering the house from where little Johnny has crawled around eating, or the smell of dirty diapers emanating from a full trash can. When someone comes to visit your home, you should be dressed in more than just a ragged pair of blue jeans and an old shirt.

She Takes Care of Her Family's Natural and Spiritual Needs

Proverbs 31:14 goes on to tell us that the virtuous woman is like the merchant ships loaded with foodstuffs; she brings her household's food from a far [country]. This woman sees that her family has the best. By serving balanced meals, she sees that they are nourished properly. She makes sure they are cared for the way they should be.

No matter how much you believe God for your child's healing, he or she will not begin to mend until you have done all you can do in the natural. Proper care is important.

Verse 15 goes on to say, "She rises while it is yet night and gets [spiritual] food for her household." "Spiritual food" is referring to intercession. Although your husband is the head of the house, you as the wife have a responsibility to intercede for your family. As I said earlier, this is one of your most important responsibilities as a wife and mother.

Intercede daily for your husband and for your children. Pray and thank the Father that you have His wisdom in every situation. Thank Him that you will say and do the right things, no matter what situation may arise. Thank Him that His promises are manifested in your home as you speak forth the Word in faith.

She Helps Her Family Increase Without Neglecting Them

Verse 16 tells us more about what the virtuous woman does for her family:

> She considers a [new] field before she buys or accepts it [expanding prudently and not courting neglect of her present duties by assuming other duties]; with her savings [of time and strength] she plants fruitful vines in her vineyard.

This Scripture could apply to women who work. Some women work because they have to; others because they enjoy it.

It is fine to have a job or career, as long as you do not neglect the duties you have already assumed as wife and mother. The key phrase in this verse is "not courting neglect of her present duties by assuming other duties." You can always find another

job, but you may not always find a peaceful and pleasant home
life. That is why you must seek God to know exactly what you
can handle so the pressures on you do not become too great.

She Girds Herself with Strength

Verse 17 tells us, "She girds herself with strength [spiritual,
mental, and physical fitness for her God-given task] and makes
her arms strong and firm." In every area of your life—spirit,
soul, and body—you become fit to do your job and then you
keep yourself fit through diligence and discipline.

You have been created to make yourself adaptable to and
suitable for someone else, and it is crucial that you gird yourself
with spiritual, mental, and physical strength. This is the only
way you will be able to fulfill the task God has given to you.

As you are faithful to keep yourself strong, verse 18 comes to
pass in your life:

> She tastes and sees that her gain from work [with and
> for God] is good; her lamp goes not out, but it burns on
> continually through the night [of trouble, privation, or
> sorrow, warning away fear, doubt, and distrust.]

You are to train your spirit to be alert to any problems that
may arise.

All the negative things listed in this verse—trouble, privation,
and sorrow—cannot take hold in your marriage and your home
when you do what you know to do. In the same way, fearful
thoughts of doubt and distrust can only lodge in your mind and

torment you when you know you're not doing what you're supposed to be doing. You may begin to wonder if your husband is doing what *he's* supposed to be doing—and that is when the battles begin.

So keep yourself strong in God. Continually draw on His grace and strength to make yourself suitable, adaptable, and completing to your husband. Then you will be able to prevent these demonic attacks from harming your marriage and your family as you follow God and His Word.

She Is Always Prepared To Help

Let's go on to verses 19 and 20:

> She lays her hands to the spindle, and her hands hold the distaff. She opens her hand to the poor, yes, she reaches out her filled hands to the needy [whether in body, mind, or spirit].

If your neighbor needs help, you should be ready to help in whatever way you can. The world says, "Don't get involved." However, you had better get involved. As a Christian, you are a love person, and love never fails. Love protects, so you do not have to worry about getting hurt.

Then verse 21 says, "She fears not the snow for her family, for all her household are doubly clothed in scarlet." This paints a picture spiritually of the divine protection afforded the family of the woman who diligently prepares for any problem that may arise.

Many times people in northern climates are caught in snow-storms and are unable to get food and other necessities. People panic because they are not prepared. They think, *What am I going to do? I have to find a way to get some groceries. We don't even have milk and bread.*

The virtuous woman never worries about the winter because she has diligently prepared for it. She knows her family will have enough food and the proper clothing to keep them warm in any situation.

You do not have to fear crises if you are doing what you know to do. When you function as the wife and mother God created you to be, your household will always have everything it needs, no matter what circumstances you may face.

She Understands Prosperity

Verse 22 goes on to tell us that the virtuous woman understands prosperity:

She makes for herself coverlets, cushions, and rugs of tapestry. Her clothing is of linen, pure and fine, and of purple [such as that of which the clothing of the priests and the hallowed cloths of the temple were made].

This woman realizes that if she is diligent and frugal, her home will have the finest. You have the right to ask the Father, "Please give me the wisdom to know how I can make my home the way I desire it to be—beautiful but 'homey.'"

One time I asked the Lord for all-wood furniture that I could afford on my budget. He answered that prayer by leading me to a bedroom suite that was exactly what I wanted and was selling for half price.

Many times we think, *First I have to find what I want. Then when I find it, I'll ask the Father if I can have it.* But that way of thinking is backwards. Go to God first, and He will lead you to your heart's desire.

As you obey what the Lord tells you to do in your life and your home, blessings will come to you in abundance. When those blessings begin to manifest, remember where they came from. Never forget that the firstfruits belong to the Lord. Do not be stingy with your money and try to hold on to it.

Many women start out trusting the Lord. However, when God begins to bless them, they become stingy. They have a continual struggle with giving because material things have become their security.

You have only one Source of security, and that is God. Everything on this earth is only temporary. If your security is in things, you are standing on shaky ground.

She Makes Her Husband Successful

Now look at what verse 23 says: "Her husband is known in the [city's] gates, when he sits among the elders of the land."

We have seen all the good things this woman does for her family. Her husband has begun to go out in this world and become successful in every area of his life because she has taken her place as a virtuous woman, wife, and mother. That is why he is known in the [city's] gates.

The husband is known largely because his wife has done her part to see that he has a happy home. She has prayed for him daily, and he has learned how to operate in the wisdom of God. As a result, verse 25 is true in this woman's life:

Strength and dignity are her clothing and her position is strong and secure; she rejoices over the future [the latter day or time to come, knowing that she and her family are in readiness for it].

She Speaks and Acts with Wisdom

Verse 26 tells us how this virtuous woman speaks to her family and to those around her:

She opens her mouth in skillful and godly Wisdom, and on her tongue is the law of kindness [giving counsel and instruction].

Notice she doesn't indulge in yelling and screaming and pushing in order to make her voice heard.

The only way this woman can accomplish all of her God-given responsibilities we have talked about is by first making the decision to fulfill verse 27:

She looks well to how things go in her household, and the bread of idleness [gossip, discontent, and self-pity] she will not eat.

I like what this verse says. The virtuous woman does not have time to eat the bread of idleness, which includes gossiping and dwelling on thoughts of discontent and self-pity, because she is too busy doing what God has called her to do.

If you are doing what God has given *you* to do, you will not have time for gossip either. You also will not have time to be discontented or to feel sorry for yourself. Instead, you will go through each day with a sense of fulfillment.

Praise Is Her Reward

Now look at verse 28:

Her children rise up and call her blessed (happy, fortunate, and to be envied); and her husband boasts of and praises her, [saying], Many daughters have done virtuously, nobly, and well [with the strength of character that is steadfast in goodness], but you excel them all.

One of the greatest pleasures I have ever had was the day my youngest daughter sent me a dozen red roses on her twenty-first birthday. The card she sent said, "Mom, I love you. Because of you, I have had a full, beautiful twenty-one years."

The first thing that came to my mind as I read this was, "Her children rise up and call her blessed" (v. 28). My daughter's words ministered to me so much. They were my reward for all the years I had endeavored to be the best mother possible according to God's Word.

Another time when I was out of town for my birthday, I received a beautiful bouquet of two dozen pink roses from my husband. Accompanying the bouquet was a precious note that said, "Even though we are apart, we are together. And 'you excel them all.'" That note confirmed to me that the Word was working in my life to make me the virtuous woman God desired me to be.

It is true that the ultimate reward for your obedience comes from the Father God. But as you are diligent to follow His plan for you as a virtuous woman of God, you will also receive a gratifying reward from those around you. They will want you to know of their love for you and their thankfulness for all you have done for them.

When these blessings begin to happen in your life, Proverbs 31 will come alive to you as never before. You'll experience an inner satisfaction that money can't buy.

Remember, Jesus was known for His works, and you are to be His light shining forth here on this earth. As you do what is at hand, caring for your husband and children as God has called you to do, the praise will come. Your husband will be proud to say, "This is my wife." Your children will be proud to say, "This is my mother." Then you can turn around and give all the glory to God, because He is the One who made you a virtuous woman.

Keep your eyes on Jesus. Stay in His Word, and spend time with Him in prayer. Then your children will rise and call you blessed, and your husband will say, "Of all the virtuous women who have walked this earth, you excel them all."

God is calling you to walk in wholeness as a woman of God. You can fulfill that call. You can be a winner in this great balancing act God is asking you to undertake. You can be the virtuous woman, wife, and mother He created you to be.

The Word of God is *truth*. Many things that are true, but only God's Word is truth. Therefore, you have to make this decision: "I will follow the report of truth. God's Word says I can be a virtuous woman, so I can. I can be a godly wife and mother according to His Word. I will walk in the fullness of God's plan for me. I will allow Him to work in me and make me that whole person He created me to be."

I urge you to grasp what I have shared with you in this book. Meditate on the Scriptures contained within these pages. Read this book once a month to learn and grow as a woman, wife, and mother. As you recognize certain areas in your life where you are failing to function in the perfection God created you to function, do whatever is necessary to make the necessary adjustments.

I know it is not always easy to change in the natural. Your spirit, which is the real you, is perfect. When you let your spirit dominate your life, change will become easy. The truth of who you are in Christ will become an inseparable part of you, and you will begin to flow in your role as a godly woman the way God always intended for you to do.

I have learned that the Word of God is actually very simple. Our natural way of thinking makes it seem difficult. God created us to love Him. He created us to understand and to

THE VIRTUOUS WOMAN REVEALED

know Him. So as we seek Him first in our lives, everything else He has asked us to do becomes easy.

Sometimes you may try to second-guess yourself by wondering, *Have I really done everything I should have done?* Although you may not have attained the perfection you desire, at least you are not sitting back and saying, "Well, until I know I can do all this perfectly, I'm not going to do anything."

Allow the Scriptures that abide within you to rise and become life to you. You are walking in the Word to the best of your ability. Therefore, you *will* reap the benefits of your obedience in your own life and in the lives of your family members.

God has created you to function as a godly woman, wife, and mother. He has given you everything you need to follow through and do what He has called you to do. Believe the truth of God's Word about you! As you become an adaptable, suitable, and completing helper to your husband, you will be fulfilled in your marriage. As you teach your children properly in the Word and live the Word before them, you will experience the joy of raising godly, obedient offspring.

Sure, you have been given a big responsibility, but you can walk in it. You know who you are in Christ. You understand that you can do everything God has asked you to do, but only through Christ who strengthens you.

So above all else, seek God first, intercede for and tend to your family. Abound in love, and walk in God's peace. Make it your goal to be a virtuous woman. You will realize what a joy it is to be one, whom God has so skillfully and carefully hand-crafted to be desired and admired.

Endnotes

Chapter 2

1 Wenham, p. 34.

2 Wenham, p. 87

Chapter 3

1 Strong, entry # 8444, p. 123. s.v. "deliverance"

Chapter 6

1 Strong, entry #3335, p. 51. s.v. "formed"

2 Wenham, p. 59.

3 Strong, entry #1129, p. 22. s.v. "banah"

4 *The Old Testament Study Bible,* "Genesis," p. 33.

5 Strong, entry # 5829, p. 87. s.v. "help"

6 Strong, entry #5046, p. 76. s.v. "meet"

7 Strong, entry # 1692, p. 29. s.v. "cleave"

8 Webster.

9 Ibid.

10 Ibid.

11 Ibid.

12 Strong, entry #5849, p. 87. s.v. "crown"

13 *The Oxford Dictionary and Thesaurus,* p. 341

14 Webster.

Chapter 8

1 *The Oxford Dictionary and Thesaurus,* p. 447.

Chapter 9

1 Strong, entry #7836, p. 114.

2 *The Old Testament Study Bible,* "Proverbs, Ecclesiastes, Song of Solomon,"* p. 123.

References

Strong, James. *The Hebrew and Chaldee Dictionary,"* *The New Strong's Exhaustive Concordance of the Bible.* Nashville: Thomas Nelson Publishers, 1990.

The Old Testament Study Bible. Springfield: World Library Press, Inc., 1994.

The Oxford Dictionary and Thesaurus. New York: Oxford University Press, 1996.

Webster, Noah. *American Dictionary of the English Language.* 1828.

Wenham, Gordon J. "Genesis 1-15" *Word Biblical Commentary.* Waco: Word Books, 1987.

About the Author

If one phrase could describe the life and ministry of Pat Harrison, it would be "I love the Holy Spirit." Anytime she makes that statement, Pat goes on to say, "I love the Holy Spirit because He is everything to me the Father said He would be."

Throughout her life and walk with God, Pat has learned that God is faithful and that the Word of God is true. With her husband, Buddy, they have been pastors, built successful businesses, and led an international ministry. Pat learned anew how faithful God is when Buddy went home to be with the Lord in November 1998. She has continued to be involved with directing the businesses, leading the ministry, and traveling and sharing the truth of God's Word.

She is a successful author, speaker, and leader. Her insights into the Word of God and her lifelong personal walk with the Holy Spirit are an inspiration to those she ministers to and touches with her life.

Pat has written several books that have been distributed throughout the world. Her writings and ministry encourage people to develop a personal walk with God and get to know the person of the Holy Spirit.

For a list of cassette tapes
by Pat Harrison
or for other information
regarding her ministry,
write:

Pat Harrison

P. O. Box 35443

Tulsa, OK 74153

*Please include your prayer requests
and comments when you write.*

Books by Pat Harrison

Overflowing With the Holy Spirit:
Know the Person of the Holy Spirit and
Learn To Walk in His Power

The Great Balancing Act:
Finding Joy as a Woman, Wife, and Mother

Available from your local bookstore.

Prayer of Salvation

A born-again, committed relationship with God is the key to a victorious life. Jesus, the Son of God, laid down His life and rose again so that we could spend eternity with Him in heaven and experience His absolute best on earth. The Bible says, "For God so loved the world, that he gave his only begotten Son, that whosoever believeth in him should not perish, but have everlasting life" (John 3:16).

It is the will of God that everyone receive eternal salvation. The way to receive this salvation is to call upon the name of Jesus and confess Him as your Lord. The Bible says, "That if thou shalt confess with thy mouth the Lord Jesus, and shalt believe in thine heart that God hath raised him from the dead, thou shalt be saved. For whosoever shall call upon the name of the Lord shall be saved" (Romans 10:9,13).

Jesus has given salvation, healing, and countless benefits to all who call upon His name. These benefits can be yours if you receive Him into your heart by praying this prayer:

Heavenly Father, I come to You admitting that I am a sinner. Right now, I choose to turn away from sin, and I ask You to cleanse me of all unrighteousness. I believe that Your Son, Jesus, died on the cross to take away my sins. I also believe that He rose again from the dead so that I may be justified and made righteous through faith in Him. I call upon the name of Jesus Christ to be the Savior and Lord of my life. Jesus, I choose to follow You, and I ask that You fill me with the power of the Holy Spirit. I declare right now that I am a born-again child of God. I am free from sin, and full of the righteousness of God. I am saved, in Jesus' name. Amen.

If you have prayed this prayer to receive Jesus Christ as your Savior, or if this book has changed your life, we would like to hear from you. Please write us at:

Harrison House Publishers
P.O. Box 35035
Tulsa, Oklahoma 74153

You can also visit us on the web at
www.harrisonhouse.com

The Harrison House Vision

Proclaiming the truth and the power

Of the Gospel of Jesus Christ

With excellence;

Challenging Christians to

Live victoriously,

Grow spiritually,

Know God intimately.